# Essential Photoshop® 5 for Web Professionals

ISBN 0-13-012833-3

9 780130 128331

## Other Books in the Series

- *Essential CSS & DHTML for Web Professionals*
  Dan Livingston and Micah Brown

- *Essential JavaScript for Web Professionals*
  Dan Barrett, Dan Livingston, and Micah Brown

- *Essential Perl 5 for Web Professionals*
  Micah Brown, Chris Bellew, and Dan Livingston

# Essential Photoshop 5 for Web Professionals

### Brad Eigen
*MadBoy Productions*

### Dan Livingston
*Wire Man Productions*

### Micah Brown
*Etail Enterprises*

Prentice Hall PTR
Upper Saddle River, NJ 07458
http://www.phptr.com

**Library of Congress Cataloging-in-Publication Data**

Eigen, Brad.
  Essential Photoshop 5 for Web professionals / Brad Eigen, Dan Livingston,
Micah Brown.
       p. cm -- (Prentice Hall essential Web professionals series)
    ISBN 0-13-012833-3 (pbk.)
    1. Computer graphics.  2. Adobe Photoshop.  3. Web sites--Design.
I. Livingston, Dan.  II. Brown, Micah.  III. Title.  IV. Series.
T385.E395    1999
006.6'869--dc21                                   99-16800
                                                     CIP

Editorial/Production Supervision: Benchmark Productions, Inc.
Acquisitions Editor: Karen McLean
Cover Design Director: Jerry Votta
Cover Design: Scott Weiss
Cover Illustration: Jean Francois Podevin, from *The Stock Illustration Source, Vol. 5*
Manufacturing Manager: Alexis R. Heydt
Editorial Assistant: Audri Anna Bazlen
Marketing Manager: Dan Rush
Project Coordinator: Anne Trowbridge

© 2000 Prentice Hall PTR
Prentice-Hall, Inc.
Upper Saddle River, NJ 07458

Prentice Hall books are widely used by corporations and government agencies for
training, marketing, and resale.

The publisher offers discounts on this book when ordered in bulk quantities.
For more information, contact: Corporate Sales Department, Phone: 800-382-3419;
Fax: 201-236-7141; E-mail: corpsales@prenhall.com; or write: Prentice Hall PTR,
Corp. Sales Dept., One Lake Street, Upper Saddle River, NJ 07458.

Adobe and Photoshop are trademarks of Adobe Systems Incorporated.

Printed in the United States of America

10 9 8 7 6 5 4 3 2 1

ISBN 0-13-012833-3

Prentice-Hall International (UK) Limited, *London*
Prentice-Hall of Australia Pty. Limited, *Sydney*
Prentice-Hall Canada Inc., *Toronto*
Prentice-Hall Hispanoamericana, S.A., *Mexico*
Prentice-Hall of India Private Limited, *New Delhi*
Prentice-Hall of Japan, Inc., *Tokyo*
Prentice-Hall (Singapore) Pte. Ltd., *Singapore*
Editora Prentice-Hall do Brasil, Ltda., *Rio de Janeiro*

# Contents

# Introduction

## ◆ Who Needs This Book?

If you are asked to create a Web site using images, and your have a limited knowledge of creating Web images with Photoshop, this book is for you. By following along while we create the two example Web sites, you will acquire the knowledge necessary to create solutions to real-life problems.

This is more than just a bible or dictionary of Photoshop terms and tools. In those types of books you have to know what the tool can do in order to look up how to do it. And if you know what the tool can do, you probably don't have to be told how to use it.

This book answers real questions such as, "How do I take the green out of facial tones?" or "Now that I have an image, how do I make it a Web image?" This is not a reference book that will sit and gather dust on your library shelf. This book will sit on the edge of your desk with Post-It notes or bookmarks sticking out of your favorite pages. This book shows you how to get the job done.

# ◆ How This Book Is Laid Out

You will follow along as two Web sites are created using Photoshop. Each chapter starts with a problem that requires a quick solution. We don't just point to the tools in Photoshop. We take you through each step, showing you several different ways to fix the problems. There are also exercises at the end of each chapter so you can practice the different techniques you learn.

# ◆ The Projects

We'll be creating Web sites for two different types of companies. The first is Shelley Biotechnologies, a fast-growing biotech start-up. We've been asked to create a corporate site without many frills in the design area. The second company is *Stitch*, an online fashion magazine. This project is a little more fun in the design area. Both Web sites present unique problems. Work alongside us as we take you through projects that allow you ample time and some that are deadline-sensitive.

# ◆ An Introduction to Photoshop

Adobe® Photoshop is the best image-editing software available. If you can imagine it, you can do it with Photoshop. Photoshop is pixel-based software—that means that every image is made up of tiny little squares. If you zoom in as far as you can on any image in Photoshop, you will see that the picture is created with many little squares of color. Some drawing programs such as Illustrator® or Freehand® are vector-based, which means they can draw a perfect circle. Those applications assign the mathematical coordinates to each piece of the line. In order to manipulate those lines, you must move or alter the line segment. In Photoshop, you manipulate one pixel or square at a time. When you draw a circle it has to be made up of squares, and many little squares appear to be a perfect circle. Photoshop is a very powerful tool. In fact, almost every image you see in magazines and catalogs has been altered or manipulated in Photoshop.

Go ahead and jump in! Turn the page and begin learning your Photoshop Web essentials.

# Acknowledgments

## ◆ Brad Eigen

I would like to thank all those that I love, especially my best friend and wife Jeanette; my dad Richard and his wife Wendy; my sister Darci; my mother Charlyne; and my friends, Shane, Jon, Mark, Ken, and Matt for continuing to inspire me and remind me what life is about.

Special thanks go to Jeanette for putting up with the continuous interruptions that came with writing this book and running a business in the same office during the year she wrote her master's thesis. Jeanette, I'm very lucky to have you as a partner.

I would also like to thank Dan Livingston and Micah Brown for allowing me to be a part of this exciting *Essential Web* series.

## ◆ Dan Livingston

We had the good luck to work with Mark Taub and Karen McLean from Prentice Hall on this project. We especially tested Karen's cattle-herding skills, and she remained remarkably patient and focused throughout the process.

I would like to thank my fiancée, Tanya Muller, for her continuing patience and encouragement. I wouldn't have been able to write this book while starting my own business without her by my side. Her support was, and continues to be, invaluable.

I'd also like to thank W. Bradley Scott of Clear Ink for coming up with the idea of using an online fashion magazine as a fictional company. He also acted as technical reviewer, and was generally very helpful.

Finally, I'd like to thank my design mentor, Brad Eigen of MadBoy Productions. He's the Daddy.

## ◆ Micah Brown

I would like to give special thanks to my wife, Dawn, who has helped me in too many ways to mention. You are my love, my life, and most importantly, my best friend. I dedicate this book to her and our daughter, Ashley Nova, who has yet to be born into this world—we can't wait to meet you!

Also a special thanks to my parents, William and Donna, and my extended parents, Beppe and Joy, for everything they have done for me these last 29 years. I wouldn't be the person I am today if it weren't for them. I will always be grateful for how much you all have taught me through the years and helped me to grow as a person.

Thanks to Mark Taub and Karen McLean for helping Dan and me get this book series out of our brains and onto paper. You are right, this is a little tougher than we had first imagined! Also, thanks to Carl Gorman, my partner in crime at Etail Enterprises (www.etail.com), and my band members, Kelly and Carl from Nitrus, for putting up with me through all of this.

Finally, thanks to my co-authors Brad Eigen and Dan Livingston, as well as all the others who worked on the books in this series. If it weren't for you, I wouldn't be writing this.

# About the Authors

## ◆ Brad Eigen

Brad Eigen has been immersed in the World Wide Web since 1994. His artistic background, including a masters degree in fine arts, an undergraduate degree in journalism, and his experience as a photojournalist, were all instrumental in transferring his love of art to the Internet. Brad's years of print design in the corporate world and his insatiable appetite for the culture of the Web have led him to become an expert in accessible, professional designs. His Web design has been honored by the Web Marketing Association's Standard of Excellence Award, and he has been honored for his print work with *Print Magazine's* Award of Design Excellence for software and hardware packaging. Brad has also been a speaker at Adobe Internet conferences around the country. He currently runs his own design company, MadBoy Productions.

# ◆ Dan Livingston

Coming from a background in marine biology, Dan Livingston was drawn to Web design in early 1996. His Web sites have since included high-profile clients such as Apple, Pacific Bell, and Novell. His sites have won numerous awards, and have been featured both in design books and on *CNN Prime Time*. His envelope-pushing DHTML site, Palette Man, has received international recognition, as well as "Cool Site" awards from Yahoo!, Macromedia, and *USA Today*. Dan was a Web designer and scripter at Web design firm Clear Ink before starting his own successful design/user interface company, Wire Man Productions. He continues to produce titles for Prentice Hall's *Essential* series.

# ◆ Micah Brown

After working in the print industry for several years, Micah Brown started his career with the Web industry back in 1995 as both a programmer and designer. Some of the sites Micah has under his belt are Dr. Laura, Pacific Bell, Amazing Discoveries, and Ascend Communications.

Micah has also been a technical reviewer for Prentice Hall for the last three years for various publications, most notably *Perl by Example* by Ellie Quigley.

Micah is currently a co-owner of Etail Enterprises, a Web consulting firm located in southern California that specializes in bringing companies into this new arena of online advertising.

# 1 Basic Doodling

## IN THIS CHAPTER

- The Big Projects
- Task: Create a Secondary Page Template for Shelley Biotechnologies
- Creating a New Document
- Dealing with Layers
- Paint Bucket and Color
- Placing and Editing Text
- Rulers, Guides, Moving, and Linking
- Drawing Lines
- Recap
- Advanced Projects

*Welcome to Photoshop! This is the most widely used image-editing program in the world, and few designers can get by without it. It's incredibly powerful and filled with all sorts of features and goodies. In this book, we'll look at what you need to know in order to start creating images for the Web. Since much of Photoshop is geared toward print designers, we'll skip all the print-specific stuff and deal with only what Web designers need to know.*

*Many of you reading this book are people who have been assigned to take care of the company Web site. Someone saw you open Photoshop once, and for that discretion, you have been deemed the "Keeper of the Web." Several of the examples in this book are aimed directly at you "Keepers of the Web" and all the seemingly impossible tasks that your bosses move to "Priority 1" each day.*

*We're looking exclusively at Photoshop 5 because it has been on the market for almost a year, and has some significant feature enhancements over version 4. (If you haven't upgraded to version 5.0.2, you should do so now—it fixes some problems that version 5 has with rendering text. Go to Adobe's Web site at http://www.adobe.com to download the upgrade.)*

*The best way to learn Photoshop (besides reading this book, of course) is to experiment and play. Use all the menus, try all the tools, and work your way through the filters.*

## ◆ The Big Projects

This book is divided into two sections, each focusing on completing a large project. In the first half of the book, we'll create a template for all the *secondary* pages for the Shelley Biotechnologies Web site. A secondary page is any page you see after you click on a link on the homepage (see Figure 1–1).

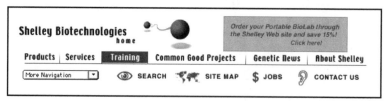

**FIGURE 1–1** The Shelley Biotech secondary page template. This is the image we'll create in the first half of this book.

We'll also be dedicating a chapter to a last-minute Photoshop emergency. Trust us, this kind of thing happens all the time.

In the second half of the book, we'll be creating the lush homepage of *Stitch*, an online fashion magazine (see Figure 1–2). More on this later.

For this chapter, however, we're just going to get used to Photoshop and build the fundamental elements of the Shelley Biotech template.

**FIGURE 1–2** The *Stitch* homepage. This is the image we'll create in the second half of the book.

## ◆ Task: Create a Secondary Page Template for Shelley Biotechnologies

Most of this chapter will be spent showing you how to move through Photoshop and deal with its basic features and floating palettes; things you absolutely have to know in order to work effectively in Photoshop. Then we'll draw the fundamental shapes and text needed for this template.

## ◆ Creating a New Document

To create a page where we can start working, simply go to the File menu and choose New. A dialog box will appear, asking you about your new document (see Figure 1–3).

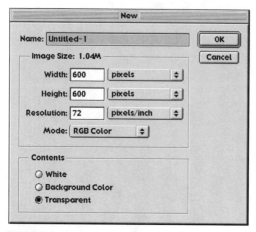

**FIGURE 1–3** The New file dialog box

Here's what to do:

1. Keep your new document untitled.

2. Make sure the dimensions are 600 pixels × 600 pixels. You may have to change the units from inches to pixels first.

3. Make sure the resolution is 72 pixels/inch. Whenever you're creating graphics for the Web, always use 72 pixels/ inch, because that's what computer monitors use. If you choose a different resolution, the final image will either be too small or too large when displayed on the Web.

4. Make sure Mode is set to RGB Color. RGB stands for Red, Green, Blue, and it's how computer monitors see color, so create all of your Web images in RGB.

5. Under Contents, make sure Transparent is selected.

6. Click OK.

7. A new window appears that looks something like Figure 1–4. The checkered squares mean that nothing's there. That's Photoshop's way of saying, "This is blank."

**FIGURE 1–4** Your new Photoshop document

## ◆ Dealing with Layers

Photoshop lets you create layers in your images, which makes the job of creating complex, interesting images much, much easier. Layers act like clear sheets of plastic that lay on top of one another, each sheet having a picture on it. When you create a new document, Photoshop gives you a clean slate with a single blank layer. You can tell how many layers you have, the names of your layers, and whether an individual layer is visible by looking at the Layers palette (see Figure 1–5).

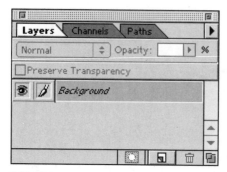

**FIGURE 1–5** The Layers palette

Double-click on the name of the only visible layer, "Layer 1." Another dialog box appears as shown in Figure 1–6 (get used to it, you'll be seeing a lot of these in Photoshop).

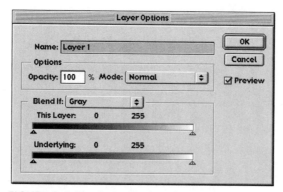

**FIGURE 1–6** The Layer Options box, where you change the layer's name

In the Name box, rename the layer "white background" and click OK. Get in the habit of specifically naming all of your layers now. When all of your layers are named something like "Layer 53," it becomes difficult to find exactly which layer had that little blue circle (or whatever) on it. There are a lot of other things you can do in this dialog box, but we're going to ignore them all. For now, just change the name.

## Deconstructing the Layers Palette

The Layers palette is important enough that you should know what all the parts of it do. We're not going to use all the pieces, but you should be familiar with them. Let's look again at the top of the palette first (see Figure 1–7).

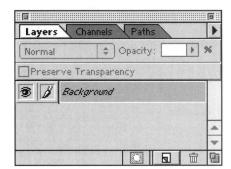

**FIGURE 1–7** Revisiting the Layers palette

**The other palettes.** The Layers palette is actually three palettes combined into one. The other two palettes are the Channels and Paths palettes. Click on the word Channels, and you'll see what looks like four layers: RGB, Red, Green, and Blue. Remember that all computer monitors see in RGB color. The Red, Green, and Blue channels contain information about how much of those three colors are in the image. The RGB layer shows the combination of all three. The Paths layer is where you use special drawing tools called *paths*. Don't worry about it for now.

**The little arrow at the right edge.** This gives you some options to manipulate your layers in several ways.

**The pull-down menu with the word "Normal" on it.** This is the Blending menu. Choosing different options determines how a layer interacts with the images on the layers below it.

**Preserve Transparency.** This deals with how filters affect certain images. We'll discuss this in Chapter 6, "The Art of the Cut."

**The eyeball.** The eye tells you that the images on that layer are visible. If there's no eyeball, everything on that layer is hidden.

**At the very bottom of the palette: the gray square with the circle in it.** This creates a layer mask over a layer. We'll cover this in Chapter 2, "Intermediate Doodling."

**At the very bottom of the palette: the page with a folded corner.** This is the New Layer icon. Clicking on this directly creates a new layer (try it). If you grab and drag a layer over this icon, it makes a copy of that layer (try it).

**At the very bottom of the palette: the trash can.** This deletes the layer. If you grab and drag a layer over this icon, it deletes it (try it).

## ◆ Paint Bucket and Color

Now we're ready for some color. The first thing we're going to do is make a white background for our image, and the tool for that job is the Paint Bucket. The Paint Bucket is used to fill in areas with a solid color. To use the Paint Bucket:

1. Click on the Paint Bucket tool in the Photoshop toolbar (see Figure 1–8).

FIGURE 1–8 The Paint Bucket tool

2. Click anywhere inside your new document.

3. Wait a minute, why is it black? (See Figure 1–9).

We need to tell the Paint Bucket to color the page white, not black. Here's how to do that:

1. Find the two rectangles of color on the toolbar. Photoshop keeps two colors readily available for all its tools—the one in front is the foreground color and the one in back is the background color (see Figure 1–10). Most tools use the foreground color.

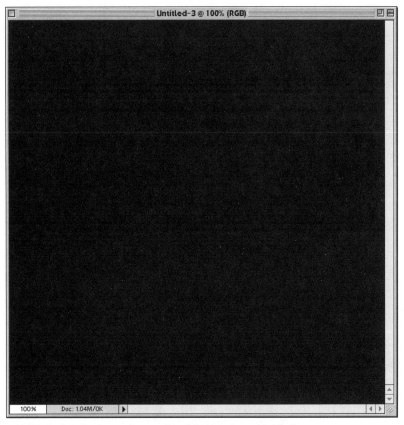

**FIGURE 1–9** Why is our image black? We wanted white!

**FIGURE 1–10** The foreground and background colors

2. Notice that black is the current foreground color and white is the current background color. We want to switch these.

3. Click on the little double-headed arrow between both colors. That switches the foreground and background colors.

4. Now that white is the foreground color, make sure the paint bucket is the selected tool, then click anywhere in your new document and your image will turn white.

Save the document (File → Save) as secondary.psd. PSD stands for Photoshop Document, and it's the standard extension to use.

## ◆ Placing and Editing Text

One of the new features of Photoshop 5 is the Text Editor, which makes creating, maintaining, and modifying text quite easy. We'll use it to create the names of the different Web site sections.

1. Click on the little double-headed arrow between the foreground and background colors to make the foreground color black.

2. Click on the Type tool in your toolbar (see Figure 1–11).

**FIGURE 1–11** The Type tool

3. Click anywhere in your document, and a dialog box pops up (see Figure 1–12).

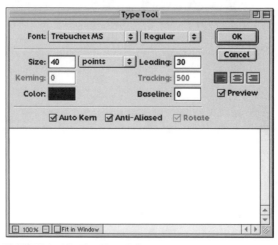

**FIGURE 1–12** The Text Editor

4. We've chosen the Trebuchet MS font. Choose any easily readable font.

5. Make the font size 10 points.

6. Don't make the font bold or italic.

7. In the big blank space, type "Products" and click OK.

8. Photoshop automatically creates a new layer with the word "Products" on it. You can tell text layers from other layers because of the big "T" next to the layer name (see Figure 1–13).

**FIGURE 1–13** A text layer

9. Repeat the preceding steps to create text layers with the following names: "Services," "Training," "Common Good Projects," "Genetic News," and "About Shelley."

10. If you misspell something or want to change anything about text on a text layer, double-click on the layer's name and the text dialog box appears. Make all of your changes there.

11. Save your file.

**Save Early and Often**

You should save your Photoshop file after making any significant changes to it. We can tell you to do this, but you probably won't until you make a lot of changes to an image and your machine crashes, losing all your hard work. Mark our words—everybody has to learn the hard way at least once.

## ◆ Rulers, Guides, Moving, and Linking

Right now, your screen looks like Figure 1–14.

We need to line these words up and space them correctly. In order to line them up, we're going to use guides, which are straight lines that Photoshop draws on the screen, but aren't part of the image. We'll use guides to line up all the words and then get rid of the guides. Here's how to use them:

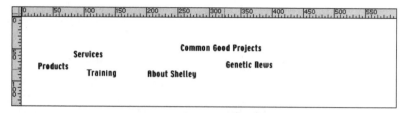

**FIGURE 1–14** Some words against a white background

1. On the menu bar, go to View → Show Rulers. Ruler measurements appear along the top and left sides of the image.

2. Click inside the ruler across the top and keep the mouse button down.

3. Drag the rule down into your image and let go of the mouse button (see Figure 1–15).

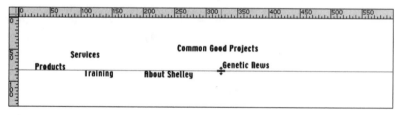

**FIGURE 1–15** Dragging a guide into the image

Violá! That blue line is a guide. If you want to move it from where it is now, select the Move tool (see Figure 1–16).

**FIGURE 1–16** The Move tool

Move the cursor over the blue line. The cursor will change to look like the following icon:

Now move the guide to the middle of your document.

We want to line up all of the words along this horizontal line. Keep the Move tool selected and click once on the Products layer. That layer will be highlighted in the Layers palette, showing that it's the current layer—anything you do will now happen on that layer. With the Move tool selected, click on your image near the word "Products," hold down the mouse button, and drag the word so that it sits on top of the guide. Do this for all of the words. Once you get the words close to where you want them to be, you can use the arrow keys to move them up, down, or across one pixel at a time (see Figure 1–17).

**FIGURE 1–17** Your current screen with the words lined up

Now that the words are lined up, we don't want to lose that alignment by accidentally moving one of them. We can keep the word in the same relative position by linking the layers. That way, if we move one layer, all the others move along with it.

Link layers by clicking in the special Link box on the Layers menu (see Figure 1–18).

**FIGURE 1–18** The Link box

Link all of the text layers as shown in Figure 1–19.

| | | About Shelley | T |
|---|---|---|---|
| | | Genetic News | T |
| | | Common Good Projects | T |
| | | Training | T |
| | | Services | T |
| | | Products | T |

**FIGURE 1–19** The linked layers

The next step is to align all of the words so they're spaced evenly. You could figure out exactly how many pixels apart each word should be, but we've found that you can get just as good a result by carefully eyeballing it. We'll leave the horizontal spacing to you (Hint: You'll have to unlink them for this part, but link them back together when you're done).

When you're finished, save. But you knew that.

## ◆ Drawing Lines

Now, let's draw those blue lines below and in between the words. We won't worry about the fading effect for now—we'll deal with that in a later chapter.

1. Since we want the lines to be blue, not black, we need to change the foreground color from black to blue. To change a foreground or background color, use the Color Picker. You can call the Color Picker by simply clicking on either the foreground or background color boxes. The Color Picker is shown in Figure 1–20.

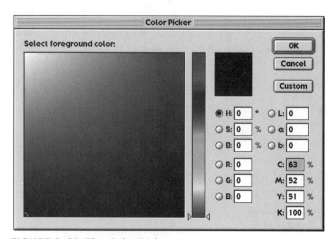

**FIGURE 1–20** The Color Picker

2. You can choose a color by moving the triangular slider up and down the rainbow stripe and dragging the little circle around.

3. You can also choose the color by manually entering numbers. In our case, we'll enter zero in the R box, 51 in the G box, and 153 in the B box (yes, the letters stand for Red, Green, and Blue, respectively). Generally, any value from 0 to 255 is acceptable.

Now that we have the color we want in the foreground, let's start drawing those lines.

1. Create a new layer by clicking the New Layer icon at the bottom of the Layers palette (see Figure 1–7).

2. Select the Line tool by clicking on the Pencil tool (see Figure 1–21).

**FIGURE 1–21** The Pencil tool

3. Hold down your mouse button and a small bar will appear with two options: the Pencil tool and the Line tool. Keeping the mouse button down, roll the cursor over the Line tool. Then let the mouse button go (see Figure 1–22).

**FIGURE 1–22** The Line tool

4. Go to the Options palette. If it isn't visible, go to Window → Show Options.

5. Enter 1 for Line Width and press Return.

6. Make sure "Anti-aliased" is not checked.

7. Make sure both arrowhead options—Start and End—are unchecked.

8. With the Line tool still selected, click on a point near the left edge of the image, keep the mouse button down, and move the cursor toward the right side of the screen.

9. You'll notice that it's pretty difficult to make that line perfectly straight. An easy way to solve this is to hold down the Shift

key while you're creating the line. Holding down the Shift key forces the line to draw straight up and down, or at 45° angles.

**10.** Let go of the mouse button when the line is about 550 pixels long. One way to tell this is to look at the Info palette (if you can't see it, go to Window → Show Info). We want the line to be exactly as long as the words in the secondary navigation.

**11.** Use the Move tool to position the line a few pixels under the navigation words.

**12.** Your image now appears as shown in Figure 1–23.

Products    Services     Training     Common Good Projects     Genetic News     About Shelley

**FIGURE 1–23** The words with a blue line

**13.** Rename the layer "long blue line" and save the file.

We have the base blue line, and now we need the little blue lines in between the words. We'll create one layer with a little blue line, and then make copies of that layer.

**1.** Create a new layer and name it "short blue line."

**2.** With the Line tool still selected and blue as your foreground color, draw a short, vertical, straight line about 20 pixels high.

**3.** Using the Move tool, position the line so that it rests on top of the long blue line and is between two of the words.

**4.** Click on the name of the layer, "short blue line," and drag the layer to the New Layer icon to copy it.

**5.** Using the Move tool, move the selected new layer in between another pair of words.

**6.** Continue this process until there are lines between each pair of words.

7. Using the Move tool, move all of the layers until you have a professional-looking arrangement. Keep working until you have something that looks right to you.

## RECAP

We just created part of the secondary page for the Shelley Bio-technologies site. If you understand what we've done so far, congratulations—we've covered a lot of ground and tools quickly. The next chapter gets a little fancier, but it's nothing you can't handle.

## ADVANCED PROJECTS

1. Create the "Shelley Biotechnologies" and "home" text on your own. Note that their font sizes are different from each other and from the rest of the navigation.

2. Create the text for the common resources; that is, Search, Site Map, and so forth. The font is Helvetica and the font size is 12.

3. Create a navigation image for your own Web site.

apter

# 2 Intermediate Doodling

## IN THIS CHAPTER

- Correcting Mistakes with the History Palette
- Getting the Size Right by Scaling
- Selecting and Modifying Selections
- Fading Effects with Masking, Gradients, and Blur
- Changing Color by Filling
- How to Make a Drop Shadow
- Recap
- Advanced Projects

*You've finished creating the secondary template and now you present it to the boss as a work in progress. It's been your experience that nothing ever gets by the boss on the first pass. There are some changes for you to make to your template. The boss likes the basic concept, but wants to have individual pieces of the art modified.*

*The task at hand is to complete this piece so you can get it ready to be put on the Web. Your boss looks at it and tells you that the sizes of some of the images are off, and that some of the colors are just not right. He also wants the text to leap off the screen a little more.*

*Bring your Photoshop image back up on the screen and we'll show you how to modify things to meet the design requests.*

## ◆ Correcting Mistakes with the History Palette

When creating images in Photoshop, it's nearly impossible to remember exactly what you did and in what order—the creative mind is often different from the organized mind. Photoshop provides a little help for the purely creative mind in the form of the History palette (see Figure 2–1). The History palette allows you to view, in order, everything you've done to an image. With your image open, go to the top menu bar and select Window→History. A palette will pop up and show you each step you took in creating this image. This is one way of making changes to your image.

1. Click on any of the steps in the history to bring you right to that step.

2. Make the change you need right there in the History palette.

3. If necessary, create a new step along the way.

Remember, the History palette will give you only the history of the document from the time it was last opened. When you close the document, the history information disappears.

There are many other ways to make the changes you need. We prefer to go directly to the layer and make the changes there. Remember to give your layers names that are easily recognizable. We promise, this is one step that will make your life easier. Creating Web page graphics can grow the layers upwards of 50 or more. Just looking at a little thumbnail won't always give you the information you need. Having an accurate name makes your life easier when making revisions (and yes, there will be revisions).

## ◆ Getting the Size Right by Scaling

You've been asked to make some of the elements smaller, some larger, and some just stretched out a little—we'll use the same technique to accomplish all three. Remember that scaling an

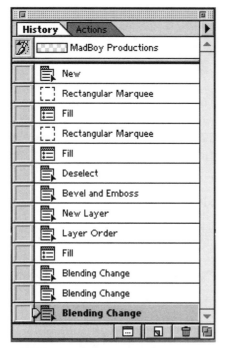

**FIGURE 2–1** The History palette in Photoshop is very useful

image in any direction will result in a change or loss of quality. This is not so with text layers.

1. Pick one of the elements from the image you created in the first chapter.

2. Click on its layer in the Layers palette.

3. Now you will be working with that object and that layer only.

4. Go to the top menu bar and select Edit→Free Transform or just hold down the Command key and press T; for a PC, hold down the Control key and press T.

5. You will see a bounding box with a center point, end points, and middle-line segment points (see Figure 2–2).

6. With Free Transform you can move the item by placing your cursor in the box and dragging it to the desired position.

**FIGURE 2–2** The Transform bounding box looks like this

   **7.** You can rotate the object by placing your cursor outside the bounding box and clicking and moving in any direction.

   **8.** You can skew an object (we'll talk about that later).

   **9.** You can also scale an object.

   **10.** To scale an object disproportionately, place your cursor on one of the corner points of the bounding box and click and move that box in or out. You will see the size of the object get larger or smaller depending on how you move.

   **11.** To scale an object proportionately, hold down your Shift key and then grab the corner point again. As you move it in or out, you will see that the object scales proportionately. Most often, this is the technique you will want to use.

## ◆ Selecting and Modifying Selections

In almost every Photoshop project, you'll need to make selections. You'll need to do this to be able to affect an object with filters or just remove the background from an image. There are many different types of selections. You can use the Rectangular Marquee tool, Elliptical Marquee tool, Single Row Marquee tool, Single Column Marquee tool, Fixed-Size Marquee tool, Lasso tool, Polygonal Lasso tool, Magnetic Polygonal Lasso tool, and Magic Wand tool. Each has a specific job in the selection process.

The Marquee tool contains all the options for using the marquee. By holding down your cursor over the tool, you will see five options (see Figure 2–3). They are, in order, the Rectangular Marquee tool, Elliptical Marquee tool, Single Row Marquee tool, Single Column Marquee tool, and a Cropping tool (we'll talk about cropping later). Simply put, a marquee is just surrounding an area with a set shape.

Try the following:

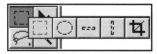

**FIGURE 2-3** All the Marquee tool options

1. Select the Rectangular Marquee tool (see Figure 2-4).

**FIGURE 2-4** The Rectangular Marquee tool

2. Place your cursor on your image and drag to see what the Rectangular Marquee tool does.

3. You will see a rectangle and a selected area.

4. Try setting a fixed size in the Marquee Tool palette. See what happens to the marquee when you click on an image.

Now try the Elliptical Marquee tool (see Figure 2-5).

**FIGURE 2-5** The Elliptical Marquee tool

1. Go to the Marquee tool in the toolbar and hold down your cursor until you see all the options. Select the Elliptical Marquee.

2. Place your cursor on your image and drag to see what the Elliptical Marquee tool does.

3. You will see an ellipse and a selected area.

### Single Row and Single Column Marquees

1. Select either of the Single Marquees (see Figure 2-6).

2. Click anywhere on your image.

3. You will see either a horizontal or vertical selected single-pixel line.

**FIGURE 2–6** The Single Row Marquee tool

4. You can use this to create a grid or just straight lines quickly without using the Pencil or Line tool.

5. Select a color from the Color palette.

6. Click on the image with one of the Single Marquees.

7. Fill the line with a color by holding down the Option key and pressing Delete.

8. See how quickly and easily you can create a line. You can use this in conjunction with the guides you learned about in Chapter 1.

Before we move on to the Lasso or Magic Wand, there are some modifiers to the Marquee tools.

### Draw a Perfect Circle or Square

1. Select either the Elliptical or Rectangular Marquee tool.

2. Place your cursor on your image.

3. Hold down the Shift key and drag your cursor.

4. You will see a perfectly constrained object.

Often times you'll want to draw a rectangle or ellipse from an exact point. As you saw when you experimented with the Rectangular and Elliptical Marquee tools, the tool will select from the upper left to the bottom right. To select from the center out, hold down the Option/Alt key (on a Mac, it's the Option key; on a PC, it's the Alt key). Try it.

### Start the Square or Circle from the Center

1. Select either the Rectangular or Elliptical Marquee.

2. Place your cursor on the image.

3. Hold down the Option/Alt key and drag your cursor.

4. You will see an object drawn from the center out.

### One More Modification

1. While holding down the Option/Alt key, press the Shift key.

2. Click and drag the cursor and you will see a perfectly constrained object drawn from the center out.

Those are just some of the many ways to select with the Marquee tools. Let's move on to the Lasso tools.

The Lasso tool is a freehand tool that allows you to create a selection that is not constrained to a set object such as a rectangle. Hold down your cursor over the Lasso tool icon. You will see three options: the Lasso, the Polygonal Lasso, and the Magnetic Polygonal Lasso (see Figure 2–7). Each has a specific function.

**FIGURE 2–7** All the Lasso tool options

### Lasso Tool

1. Select the Lasso tool (see Figure 2–8).

**FIGURE 2–8** The Lasso tool

2. Put your cursor on an image and draw around it.

3. You can close the selection yourself by drawing to where you started, or you can just let go and it will close for you.

4. By holding down the Option/Alt key, you can make the Lasso tool perform like the Polygonal Lasso tool.

### Polygonal Lasso Tool

1. Select the Polygonal Lasso tool (see Figure 2–9).

**FIGURE 2–9** The Polygonal Lasso tool

2. Put your cursor on an image and click on points along the edge of that image.

3. You will see that this tool draws in line segments.

4. To close the selection, either draw to where you began or double-click anywhere in the process. The tool will draw a line segment from your beginning point to the place at which you ended.

## Magnetic Polygonal Lasso Tool

This tool allows you to select the edges of an image without being exact.

1. Create a colored rectangle using the methods you've already learned.

2. Select the Magnetic Polygonal Lasso tool (see Figure 2–10).

**FIGURE 2–10** The Magnetic Polygonal Lasso tool

3. Put your cursor near the edge of the image and click once.

4. Continue around the rectangle, clicking close to the edges.

5. Click on your beginning point.

You will see that the selection around the rectangle is exact without your having to zoom in and make sure you are exactly on the line.

## The Magic Wand Tool

We're now going to show you one of the coolest tools ever invented in an image-editing program, but first, here's a little information on the Magic Wand tool (see Figure 2–11). The Magic Wand is a selection tool that allows you to click once and select an area that is similar in color. It can be used to select solid objects in one click or to remove the background from an image. Jump right in and try it.

**FIGURE 2–11** The Magic Wand tool

1.  Select the Magic Wand tool.

2.  Click on the rectangle you created earlier with the Magnetic Polygonal Lasso tool.

3.  You will see the entire object selected in one click.

Double-click on the Magic Wand tool and look at the Options palette (see Figure 2–12). You can set the tolerance that the Magic Wand uses by choosing between 0 and 255 pixels. A lower tolerance selects colors that are closer to the one you clicked. A higher tolerance allows you to select a broader range of colors.

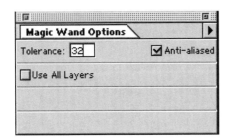

**FIGURE 2–12** The Magic Wand Options palette

### Removing a Background

1.  Open an image with a shadow or with a background that you wish to remove.

2.  Select the Magic Wand tool.

3.  Set your tolerance according to the image. Start with a low tolerance.

4.  Start clicking around the image and deleting the background.

5.  See how quickly and easily the Magic Wand tool can work.

### Some Additional Tips on Making Selections

Once you've selected a particular area, you may need to add or remove a little extra from the selection. There is a better way than starting over.

### ADDING TO THE SELECTION

1. Select the Lasso tool.

2. Place your cursor on your image and create a random selection.

3. Hold down the Shift key and lasso an area that includes a part of your current selection.

4. You will see that the Shift key allows you to add to your selection.

### SUBTRACTING FROM THE SELECTION

1. With the current selection made, hold down the Command/Ctrl key (on a Mac, it's the Command key; on a PC, it's the Ctrl key).

2. Lasso an area within the current selection.

3. You will see that area removed from your selection.

## ◆ Fading Effects with Masking, Gradients, and Blur

You have the perfect image and now your boss tells you that the square edge doesn't fit the company image—a fuzzy or blended edge is needed for the project. Don't worry, you don't have to start from scratch. Let's go to your image and see what we can do.

### Fuzzy Edges

1. Duplicate the layer of the image and it will add the word *copy* to the name.

2. Double-click the Rectangular Marquee tool.

3. Set the Feather Options to 8 in the Options palette (see Figure 2–13).

4. Click back to your image.

5. Select the image just inside the actual border.

6. Go to your top menu bar and select Select→Inverse.

7. Press Delete several times until the desired fuzzy effect is achieved.

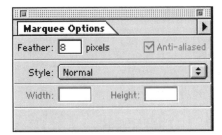

**FIGURE 2–13** The Feather option

Here's a way to create an edge that's not just evenly fuzzy.

1. Hide the layer you just created.

2. Show the original image.

3. Duplicate the original layer and call it "Fun Edge 1."

4. Double-click the Quick Mask mode or press Q.

5. Click on Selected Areas.

6. Click off the Quick Mask mode by pressing Q.

7. Select the Rectangular Marquee tool.

8. Select an area starting from just inside the image edge. Leave about 1/8 to 1/4 of an inch to the edge of the image.

9. Press Q again to return to the Quick Mask mode.

10. You'll see the colored opaque, probably red, area you selected.

11. Go to the top menu bar and select Filter→Blur→Gaussian.

12. Choose 8 pixels.

13. Go to the top menu bar and select Filter→Pixelate→Crystallize.

14. Choose cell size 10.

15. Press Q again to return to normal mode.

16. Copy the selected image.

17. Press the Command, N, and Return keys to get a new window.

18. Paste the image into the new window.

19. You will see a fun new edge on your image.

20. Copy that image back into your original document.

21. Hide the other images and show the new image.

### Using the Gradient Tool to Fade

Let's say you want to fade the bottom half of your new, cool-edged image.

1. Select the layer that the new image is on.
2. Duplicate that layer and call it "Blend."
3. Click Quick Mask mode or press Q.
4. Double-click on the Gradient tool (see Figure 2–14).

**FIGURE 2–14** The Gradient tool

5. In the Options palette, select Foreground to Background.
6. With the Gradient tool, start from the bottom of the image and draw up to the midway point of the image.
7. You will see the bottom fade out. Hold down the Command key and press Z or go to your History palette and remove the last step. Keep trying it until you get the desired affect.

## ◆ Changing Color by Filling

1. Click on the layer that has the background color box.
2. Copy the layer and call it "new color."
3. Deselect the original green background.
4. Click on the Preserve Transparency box at the top of the Layers palette. This allows you to fill only the pixels on that layer, nothing else will be filled.
5. Go to your Color palette and click the color you need.
6. Go to your top menu bar and select Edit→Fill, choose Foreground, and click OK.
7. A shortcut is to hold down the Option/Alt key and press Delete. That will fill the box with the foreground color selected. Holding down the Command key and pressing Delete fills it with the background color.

8. Since your boss wanted to present several different color variations, repeat steps 1–7.

9. Do the same for two new colors.

## ◆ How to Make a Drop Shadow

A drop shadow can be just the thing to make the type appear as if it's lifted off the page. There are several ways to do this. Our favorite is the new Drop Shadow layer effect in Photoshop 5. All you do is choose the size, length, and blur of the shadow and voilá—you have a drop shadow!

1. Select any color other than black from the Color palette.

2. Use the Type tool to create the words "Drop Shadow."

3. Select the color black in the Color palette.

4. Go to your top menu bar and select Layer→Effects→Drop Shadow (see Figure 2–15).

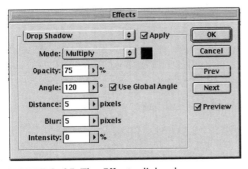

**FIGURE 2–15** The Effects dialog box

5. The Effects dialog box will present you with many different ways to create a shadow.

6. Make sure your Preview box is selected so you can see the changes on the page as they occur.

7. Try changing the different options to find one you like.

8. You can make changes to any layer after you click OK.

These shadows may give your page the added oomph that your boss wants. Try several variations.

## RECAP

In this chapter you've learned about the following tools and concepts:
- History palette
- Scaling tools
- Marquee, Lasso, and Magic Wand
- Fading effects with masking, gradients, and the pencil
- Fill
- Drop shadow

## ADVANCED PROJECTS

1. Using the masking techniques, create several fun edges for a photograph of yourself or a friend.

2. Take several images and resize them larger and smaller.

3. Take two separate images of yourself and remove the backgrounds trying each of the selection tools. Put both images of yourself on a solid colored background. Examine your edges to check your selection. Modify if necessary.

4. Change the background of your double image by using Fill.

5. Give one of your pictures a drop shadow.

6. Give the other a cast shadow.

7. Take that new image and give the edge a fade using the Gradient tool. Try other combinations and directions of the fade.

# 3 Making Images Web-Ready

## IN THIS CHAPTER

- GIF versus JPEG File Formats

- Transparency

- Interlacing

- Saving as GIF or JPEG

- Web Safe Colors and Dithering

- Animation

- Recap

- Advanced Projects

*Now that you've now created some beautiful images for the Web, the next step is to put you through Web image training camp. There are several things you need to consider before you turn your works of art into functional Web graphics. You need to make decisions on file format, color palette, optimization, transparency, interlacing, and animation. Some of the file extensions you are now familiar with are .psd (Photoshop), .pict, .tiff (Tagged Image File Format), and .eps (Encapsulated PostScript). You need to learn about two more and we will acquaint you with both—you'll be singing their praises in no time. Your new friends' names are GIF and JPEG.*

# ◆ GIF versus JPEG File Formats

There are several types of graphics file formats, but we will look at the two main Web formats: GIF and JPEG. GIF is an acronym for *Graphics Interchange Format* and is pronounced two different ways. Some users say GIF using the G from the word "graphic." Others say GIF with the G from "giraffe"—either way, it stands for the same thing. It's fun to listen to a conversation between two people who use different pronunciations. Both begin by holding fast to their style and then somewhere in the conversation one or the other switches accidentally and then corrects it later in the sentence. Good thing it's not up for Congressional debate.

JPEG is an acronym that stands for *Joint Photographic Experts Group* and is universally pronounced "Jay-peg."

Why GIF versus JPEG? It's simple. Graphics are simply too big to put on the Web as they are; you need to compress them. All browsers can read GIF and JPEG file formats. Which format is better? Let's look at the questions you'll need to ask before choosing between the two. How small do you need your image to be? How do you want the image to download? How fast do you want the image to download, and what type of image are you using? An easy way to determine which format to use is to learn what each offers. A general rule is that if you have graphics, use GIF; if you have a photograph, use JPEG. There are, however, many specifics to each format that will fill in the details of what you need. We'll give you a checklist at the end of this section so you can see which file format works best. In the meantime, here is a description of each of the formats.

## GIF

The GIF format has many advantages. If you are using graphics, type images, line drawings, or images with large blocks of color, GIF is a good choice. Following are the advantages and disadvantages of the GIF format. Terms such as *transparency, interlacing,* and *animation* will be explained in more detail later in the chapter.

### ADVANTAGES

- Loss-less compression—no image data lost in translation
- Interlacing
- Transparency
- Animation available

- Works in RGB (Red-Green-Blue) mode and converts to Index Color
- 256 colors or less
- Good for large fields of color

### DISADVANTAGES

- Creates banding on photographs and continuous tone images
- Only 256 colors
- Image dithering without Web-safe colors

## JPEG

Following are the advantages and disadvantages of the JPEG format:

### ADVANTAGES

- Lossy compression—some image data is lost (don't let that worry you)
- Settings to control amount of image loss
- Best for continuous tone images (photos, blends, gradations)
- Can use thousands or millions of colors

### DISADVANTAGES

- Not good for graphics, line drawings, or type images
- No image transparency
- No image interlacing
- No animation

# ◆ Transparency

No matter the shape of the image inside the graphic, the actual document will always be some form of a rectangle—this is where *transparency* comes in. Transparency allows you to mask out colors so they are not seen in the browser. This gives the illusion that you have a nonrectangular image on a page (see Figure 3–1).

1. Create a new document that is 2 inches × 2 inches and make the first layer blue.

2. On a separate layer, create a red square.

**FIGURE 3–1** Transparency: The original, how it looks in Photoshop with transparency, and how it looks in the browser

3.  From the top menu bar, select Image→Mode→Indexed Color.

4.  You will be asked if you want to flatten the image.

5.  Click OK and remember not to save your image when you close the document.

6.  A box will then appear asking what type of palette and how many bits and colors (see Figure 3–2).

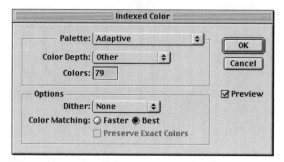

**FIGURE 3–2** The Indexed Color dialog box

7.  Click OK.

8.  From the top menu bar select File→Export→GIF89a Export (see Figure 3–3).

9.  You will be presented with your image and all its colors in the palette.

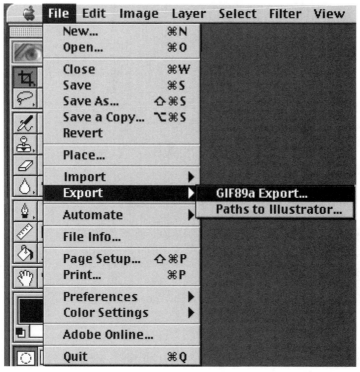

**FIGURE 3–3** Selecting GIF89a Export

10. Move your cursor over the image and click on the blue background.

11. You will see the color you selected as the transparency color, and there will be a black border around that color in the palette (see Figure 3–4).

12. Select the colors you want to be masked out.

13. Save the file.

14. Put the image on an HTML page with a black background.

15. See how the transparency works.

**FIGURE 3–4** The GIF89a Export dialog box presents your image and all its colors in the palette

# ◆ Interlacing

An image can be revealed in a browser one of two ways: It can come in one line at a time until the whole image is revealed; or it can be downloaded so that it all comes in at once, starting out a little fuzzy and then slowly sharpening. The second method can be done with the Interlacing option. Interlacing allows approximately every seventh line to show, and then the next seven. In other words, it shows lines 1, 7, 14, 21, 28, and so on, and then the next pass shows lines 2, 8, 15, 22, 29, and so on, until the image is complete. This gives the effect of venetian blinds when an image is coming in. Remember that when you are working with animated images, you don't want to save in this option for each individual cell. More on that later.

# ◆ Saving as GIF or JPEG

Now that you have enough information to decide what type of format you want to use, let's look at how to create GIFs and JPEGs. There are several methods; however, only a few will be discussed here. Let's start with the Photoshop image of a headline for the *Stitch* online fashion magazine. The header is currently in a file with the .psd Photoshop extension (see Figure 3–5). We'll save this as a GIF file because it meets all the criteria of what images work best as GIFs. There are many methods of optimizing images in the GIF or JPEG format, and Photoshop does both wonderfully. There are other programs that can be used just as compression packages and are known for getting files sizes to an absolute minimum, such as ImageReady (also from Adobe), Fireworks (from Macromedia), and DeBabelizer (from Equilibrium). You are free to use any method you want. The Photoshop methods will be covered in this book.

**FIGURE 3–5** The *Stitch* headline graphic

## Creating a GIF

1. Make sure the image you choose to work with is in RGB mode.

2. From the top menu bar select Image→Mode→RGB.

3. From the top menu bar select File→Export→GIF89a Export.

4. Make sure the Adaptive palette is selected.

5. If the number in the box is 256, change it to 255 (see Figure 3–6).

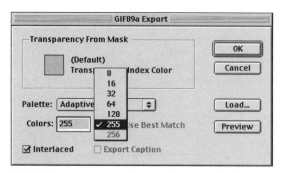

**FIGURE 3–6** Selecting the number of colors for your GIF image

6.  If the number is lower than 256, then leave it as is.

7.  Preview it if you wish by clicking Preview (it's not always an accurate preview).

8.  You will be prompted to save the document somewhere on your computer.

9.  Click OK and you have completed the simplest form of creating a GIF image.

10. Test the image by dragging it onto your open Web browser.

### Creating a JPEG

1.  Make sure your image is in RGB, CMYK, or Grayscale mode.

2.  From the top menu bar select File→Save A Copy.

3.  Change the name of the file suffix to .jpg or .jpeg.

4.  Below the filename is a Format button.

5.  Click and hold down your mouse button over the Format button (see Figure 3–7).

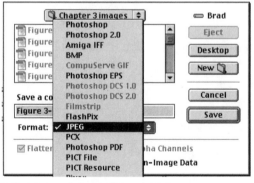

**FIGURE 3–7** Selecting the JPEG format

6.  Select JPEG format.

7.  Click Save.

8.  A JPEG Options dialog box will pop up (see Figure 3–8).

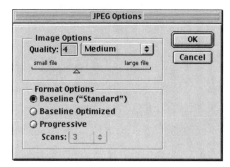

**FIGURE 3–8** Selecting a low, medium, or high quality JPEG

9. Choose Low, Medium, High, or Maximum, or move the slider to get the same results.

10. Under Format Options, select Baseline ("Standard").

11. Click OK to save the file.

12. Test the image by dragging it onto your open Web browser.

## ◆ Web Safe Colors and Dithering

When using GIF images, you are limited to 256 colors. If you are creating images on a PC, you have one set of 256 colors. If you are creating on a Mac, you have another set of 256 colors. The two types of computers share only 216 of those 256 colors. Those colors have been used to create the Web Safe palette or Web 216 palette. This option became available in Photoshop 5.

1. From the top menu bar select Window→Show Swatches.

2. From the Swatches palette, select Replace Swatches (see Figure 3–9).

3. Your computer will prompt you to find the Photoshop folder.

4. It's in the folder Goodies→Color Palettes→Web Safe Colors.

5. Select Web Safe Colors and click OK.

6. This will replace the palette with the 216 safe colors.

Using this palette will prevent your colors from *dithering* on solid areas. Dithering occurs when your computer can't display the color due to the 256-color limitation, so it tries its best to guess

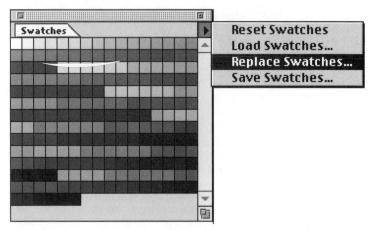

**FIGURE 3–9** Selecting Replace Swatches from the Swatches palette

at a combination of safe colors that will result in getting the color you want. In photographs, this is usually fine, but in solid-colored areas, it almost never works the way you want it to. As you know, each image is made up of pixels, or little square boxes. Zoom in on any image to see what the pixels look like.

Let's say we want a particular color blue that is not in the Web Safe Color palette. The computer will take two other colors and alternate the pixels within the color patch to try to simulate the blue you want. Sometimes the end result is fine, but often it is not. It looks grainy and it's actually a different color than what you want. See Figure 3–10 for a crude example of dithering. One square is the color you want. The second dithered square is two other colors next to each other, which, when viewed from a distance, approximate the color you want.

In order to avoid all that, use the Web Safe Color palette to select a color that each type of computer will see perfectly. That means when creating buttons, headlines, or other solid areas of color, you've got 216 colors from which to choose.

When creating gradients and blends of color, the computer will choose from the accepted amount of colors to simulate the transition area between color. That's why JPEG often works best with blends.

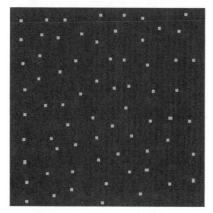

**FIGURE 3–10** A bad case of dithering

# ◆ Animation

Yes, we are talking about animation as in cartoons. Animation is simply many still images passing our eyes, and giving the illusion of movement. Like traditional animation in which each image is drawn on a cell, computer animation is the same except much quicker and easier to do. There are many tools available for creating animations for both the Macintosh and PC. Many of them are free to download such as GIF Builder for the Mac and GIF Construction Kit for the PC. Both tools can be downloaded at http://www.shareware.com. They tend to have fewer features than the animation packages included in ImageReady and Fireworks.

The basics behind animation are that you need to create each frame of the animation in Photoshop. Before you put each of your GIF layers into an animation program, you need to test it in Photoshop first. You can do this by using the layers and clicking on the eye in the Layers palette to simulate an animation. This way, you can test for any jumpiness and inconsistencies in your animation.

## RECAP

In this chapter you learned:
- The difference between GIF and JPEG images
- Advantages and disadvantages of both formats
- How to interlace an image
- How to make an image transparent
- How to save a GIF
- How to save an optimized JPEG
- What a GIF animation is
- Web Safe colors and dithering

## ADVANCED PROJECTS

1.  Take a photograph of a landscape and find the most accurate method of saving it in the smallest format.

2.  Create several headers for your Web page and find the best way to save the files between GIF and JPEG in the smallest format.

3.  Take a large image and save it two ways, as an interlaced image and without the Interlace option. Open the images in your browser and watch how they load.

4.  Create a Web page with a dark-colored background. Then use Transparency to create a nonsquare image to put on the dark background. See how that works.

5.  Create several large, colored shapes on a page and pick some Web Safe colors and some from outside the 216 palette. Save the image as both GIF and JPEG and see what each version looks like in your browser. How true are the colors from both palettes once they are saved in a .gif format?

# 4 Altering Photos

## ◆ Task: Cleaning Up the CEO's Picture

So the boss down the hall hears that you're working on the Shelley Web site and that you know Photoshop, even though at this point all you've done is open a few images and play a little. He hustles down to your cube anyway, brandishing a diskette.

"This is a photo portrait of the CEO," he grumbles. "It needs to be on our Web site in four hours, in time for the big press conference! You can clean it up, right? Great. Just make him look presentable."

You can't get out of it at this point, so you open up the image in Photoshop.

The photo is terrible. The whole image is washed out. The CEO has an ugly blemish, bloodshot eyes, a hideous yellow tie, and dark bags under his eyes. You reach for your desk, get out your passport, and look for that online airline ticket agency.

Put away your passport. You can fix this, and here's how.

When you're working with portraits, you'll probably be given an image that's a scanned photograph. Depending on who scanned it, chances are this image will be much bigger than anything you'd want to put on the Web. A good rule of thumb is to reduce the image to about 500 pixels wide (or so), work on it at that resolution, and then reduce it to Web size when you're done tweaking the image.

**NOTE**

Not too surprisingly, Macs and PCs see the world differently. In general, PC monitors are significantly darker than Mac monitors. This isn't because the monitors are built differently, but because of something called *gamma settings*. These gamma settings are determined by the computer and basically tell the monitor how bright the whites are and how dark the blacks are, as well as the value of all the colors in between. The gamma settings for PCs make them significantly darker than Macs. This is important to people who create Web images on Macs. An image that will look just right to you will probably be too dark on a PC (or darker than you would like). And at the time of writing, about 85%–90% of all computers browsing the Web are PCs, so this isn't something that Mac users can ignore.

If you're on a Mac, there is a free program you can download that will let you toggle back and forth between a Mac gamma setting and a PC gamma setting. It's called GammaToggle FKEY and you can download it off the Web at http://www.shareware.com.

## ◆ Livening Color with Brightness and Contrast

The first thing you notice about the picture is that it's washed out. All the whites are a little gray and the colors look faded and sad. Nothing's vibrant.

1. Save the original scan of the CEO and put it on a disk safely next to your passport.

2. Make a copy of the original layer.

3. Label the new layer "b/c."

4. Go to Images→Adjust→Brightness/Contrast.

5. You'll see a dialog box with two sliders (see Figure 4–1).

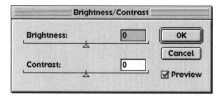

**FIGURE 4–1** Brightness/Contrast dialog box

6. Move the Brightness slider back and forth and leave it in a random place. Make sure the Preview box is checked.

7. Move the Contrast slider back and forth and notice what it does to your picture. Leave the little triangle in a random place.

8. Press the Option/Alt key and hold it down.

9. Notice how the Cancel key is now labeled "Reset." Click the Reset button. Both triangles return to their original position at 0.

10. Contrast is what will help us out in this situation. Since the image is washed out, we're going to make it look a little more alive by increasing the contrast. Start out by placing the Contrast slider at about 15 or so. Move the slider until you come to a contrast setting that looks right to you. (Be honest about how good it looks, a big part of being a graphic designer is being honest with yourself when your result doesn't really please you.)

11. On this particular image, it might look a little better if you nudge the brightness up a notch—a couple of points or so.

12. Once you have the result you want, click OK.

# ◆ Getting Rid of Blemishes by Rubber Stamping

The Rubber Stamp tool takes a piece from one section of an image and pastes it in another section. It's used mostly to clean up little imperfections in images.

1. Zoom in on a blemish and the surrounding area (see Figure 4–2).

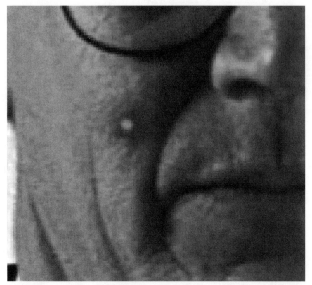

**FIGURE 4–2** The original image shows an unwanted blemish

2. What we're going to do is cover the blemish with some skin from the surrounding area—sort of a digital skin graft. That way, we get the same texture and skin tone.

3. Make a copy of the original layer.

4. Choose a smaller fuzzy-edged brush shape (see Figure 4–3). Choosing a fuzzy-edged brush will cause the skin that's already there to softly fade into the skin you'll be covering the blemish with, which will look more natural.

5. Position the Rubber Stamp icon next to the offending blemish, but not too close.

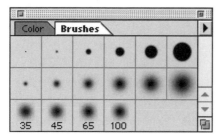

**FIGURE 4-3** The Brushes palette

6. Press the Option/Alt key and hold it down.

7. Click on the skin area.

8. Release Option/Alt.

9. Move the Rubber Stamp icon over the blemish and start painting (see Figure 4–4).

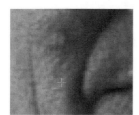

**FIGURE 4-4** Clearing the skin

Now, that looks a lot better, much better than it did before. However, it could still be improved. The skin you covered the blemish with blends in pretty well with the surrounding area, but it's not blended well enough. To make the new skin/old skin transition smoother, we'll use the Smudge tool.

## ◆ Fudging by Smudging

Often, you can't achieve perfect results unless you have a lot of time to play with the image and try some different things. But since we only have four hours to get this image to the Shelley Biotech Web site, we can get near-perfect results with the Smudge tool (see Figure 4–5).

**FIGURE 4–5** The Smudge tool

1. Make a copy of the original layer (you've heard this before).

2. Position the cursor on the border between the two areas of the skin (see Figure 4–6).

**FIGURE 4–6** Getting ready to smudge

3. Make sure your brush is small and fuzzy (see Figure 4–7).

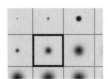

**FIGURE 4–7** Choosing a small, fuzzy brush

4. Move your brush from side to side. See what happens? It really does smudge. For this task, we won't need to smudge very much at all. Just run your mouse over the connecting areas as if you're stitching them. Make a short, quick line. Then lift up your mouse button and make another one (see Figure 4–8).

5. The CEO now has wonderful skin. Save your work.

FIGURE 4–8 Smooth, clear skin

# ◆ Lightening with the Dodge Tool

The skin looks good, but those bags under the eyes are too dark for a CEO—a programmer, fine, but not a CEO. Let's lighten them up with the Dodge tool.

FIGURE 4–9 The Dodge tool

The Dodge tool is a member of a trio: Dodge, Burn and Sponge. Dodge lightens, Burn darkens, and Sponge either makes things more colorful or fades them. We'll look at just the Dodge tool for this task. We'd only use the Burn tool to give him a black eye.

1. Select the Dodge tool.

2. Select a brush.

3. Since we don't want to completely erase his skin tone, we'll adjust the power of the Dodge tool. Go to the Options box for the Dodge tool and change the exposure to 50% (see Figure 4–10).

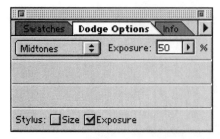

**FIGURE 4-10** The Dodge Options palette

4. Brush over the bags with quick, sure strokes. Not too much—we're just after enough lightness so that he looks healthy.

5. Now let's look at the eyes themselves. They're bloodshot and look like a freeway map.

6. Do the same thing to his eyes as you did to the bags under them. Use a smaller brush, though. Don't make his eyes too bright or they'll shine so much they'll attract attention to themselves. We want a solid entrepreneurial spirit, not a mouseketeer.

7. You just saved your work, right?

## ◆ Altering Color with Variations and the Polygonal Lasso Tool

Only one more change to the CEO is needed. Usually, one doesn't change the color of clothes in portrait photos, but his tie is the color of three-month-old mustard. Changing the color of the tie will require two steps.

1. Selecting the tie, so that when you change color, only the tie is affected.

2. Actually changing the color.

### Selecting the Tie

1. Use the sharp-edged Polygonal Lasso tool (see Figure 4–11).

**FIGURE 4–11** The Polygonal Lasso tool

2. In the Lasso Options box, enter a feather value of 2. Remember, feathering fades the edges of whatever changes you make inside the selected area.

3. Now, with the Polygonal Lasso selected, click on a section of the tie (see Figure 4–12). Don't hold down your mouse button, just click. Doing this anchors the Lasso tool. Move to the next corner on the tie and click again.

**FIGURE 4–12** Selecting the tie with the Polygonal Lasso tool

4. When you go all the way around the tie and place the Lasso icon over the original anchor point, the icon changes slightly: from ☿ to ☿. When the icon with the circle appears, click again, and the tie is selected.

## *Actually Changing the Color*

1. Go to Images→Adjust→Variations.

2. There's a lot going on in the Variations dialog box (see Figure 4–13).

3. First of all, you see the selected area, the tie. If you see more than that, you goofed. Go back and reselect the tie.

4. There's also a picture of the current tie—the original and current ties are the same right now.

5. The big color area: You can make the tie more green, yellow, cyan, red-blue, or magenta. Clicking on a color variation will alter the original. Try a bunch of different colors; this is a good place to play.

6. The lighter/darker area: Much like the big color area, you can make the original lighter or darker by clicking on one of those boxes.

7. At the top of the window, you'll see a group of three radio buttons with Shadows, Midtones, and Highlights. We are ignoring them here. Feel free to experiment on your own.

8. Also at the top of the window, you'll see a slider that goes from Fine to Coarse. We will also be ignoring this. Feel free to experiment.

9. Now that you've played with the colors some, the tie is probably some crazy color you don't actually want. Click on the Original box at the top of the screen to erase all your changes (see Figure 4–14).

10. Choose red and blue and experiment with some of the other colors until you get a tie that resembles a normal color and looks better against the CEO's suit.

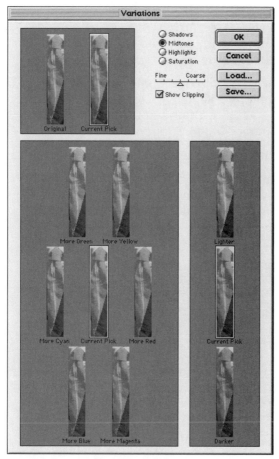

**FIGURE 4–13** The Variations dialog box allows you to view your image or selection while you adjust the color balance or contrast

**FIGURE 4–14** Clicking the Original image restores the tie to its original color

# ◆ Resizing for the Web

1. Right now the image is too big for the Web. We'll need to resize it. Save the current image.

2. Now save the image again using Save As. Save it as ceo.small.psd. Remember to look under Image→Mode to make sure it's RGB and not Index. If you resize in Index, your images will look lousy.

3. Go to Image→Image Size.

4. The Image Size dialog box lets you determine how big or small you really want the image to be (see Figure 4–15). For this picture, make sure the Constrain Proportions box is checked.

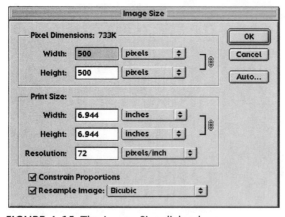

**FIGURE 4–15** The Image Size dialog box

5. How to decide how big to make the picture? Well, that depends on the layout of the Web page that will hold the picture. A pretty standard size for a portrait like this one is 100 pixels × 100–150 pixels.

6. Enter 100 in the Width box. The Height box will adjust automatically.

7. Press OK.

8. Save.

# ◆ Unsharp Mask

Sometimes resizing will make the image a little blurry. If this is the case with your image, go to Filter→Sharpen→Unsharp Mask and start experimenting with the three sliders until your image looks sharp, but not unnaturally so.

## RECAP

In this chapter you learned about the following tools and concepts:
- Brightness/Contrast
- Rubber Stamp
- Smudge
- Dodge
- Variations
- Polygonal Lasso
- Resizing
- Unsharp mask

## ADVANCED PROJECTS

Since this was such a professional job, your homework is a little more fun. Give the CEO a third eye in his forehead, but make it look really good, so that judging purely from the image, there's no reason to think the eye isn't really there. Also, give the iris an evil red tinge.

# 5 Filters and Effects

## IN THIS CHAPTER

- Task: Create the Artsy Homepage for *Stitch Magazine*
- Creating Smooth Backgrounds with the Gradient Editor
- A Cool Effect with Plastic Wrap
- Dynamic Effects with Motion Blur
- Saving Time with Eliminate White
- Useful Effects with Blur and Blending
- Recap
- Advanced Projects

## ◆ Task: Create the Artsy Homepage for *Stitch Magazine*

*Stitch Magazine* has decided on a distinct, strong visual look to separate it from the majority of the Web pages currently out there.

## ◆ Creating Smooth Backgrounds with the Gradient Editor

We want to create a simple ocean and sky for the background of the *Stitch* page. We'll use a light, slate blue for the sky and a pastel green for the water.

1. Click on the Gradient tool (see Figure 5–1).

**FIGURE 5–1** The Gradient tool

2. In the Gradient tool Options palette, click on the Edit button.

3. In the Gradient Editor dialog box, click on the New button.

4. Call this gradient "Stitch background."

5. Click on the black square in the pointer on the left-hand side to activate the gradient marker (see Figure 5–2).

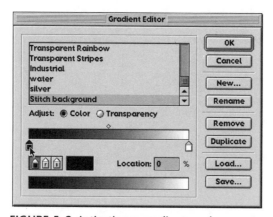

**FIGURE 5–2** Activating a gradient marker

6. Click on the color box next to the list of markers (see Figure 5–3).

7. Choose a light, slate blue.

8. Click on the pointer on the right-hand side to activate it.

9. Click on the color box and choose a green with a similar tone as your blue.

10. Click just underneath the middle of the editor bar. A new pointer appears (see Figure 5–4).

11. Click in the color box and choose white.

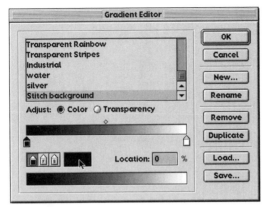

**FIGURE 5–3** The Gradient Editor's color box

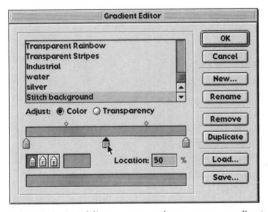

**FIGURE 5–4** Adding a new color to your gradient

12. The white will serve as a horizon, but it's too wide. Move the midpoint diamonds on the top of the editor bar toward the center (see Figure 5–5).

13. Click OK.

14. Create a new file that is 600 pixels × 600 pixels.

15. Use the Gradient tool Options palette to choose "Stitch background" and create the background (see Figure 5–6).

16. Create the background by dragging your cursor across the blank image.

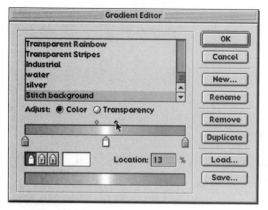

**FIGURE 5-5** Moving the midpoints

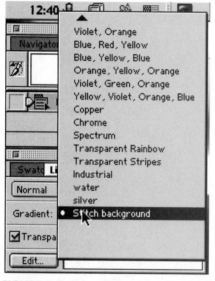

**FIGURE 5-6** Selecting your background

## ◆ A Cool Effect with Plastic Wrap

Photoshop comes with dozens of filters—some of them are great ones you use all the time and some are so weird it's hard to imagine why anyone would use them. However, it's good to familiarize yourself with all of them because even the most obtuse filters are useful sometimes (it's fun to play with them, too). Plastic Wrap, one of the stranger filters, actually comes in handy here. The background gradient in our image isn't very interesting and could use some texture.

1. Make a copy of the Gradient layer.

2. On this layer, apply Filter→Artistic→Plastic Wrap.

3. Highlight strength: 15.

4. Detail: 9.

5. Smoothness: 7.

6. Click OK and check out the new background (see Figure 5–7).

**FIGURE 5–7** The Plastic Wrap's effect

If the result isn't working for you, vary the Highlight Strength, Detail, and Smoothness sliders. Or try a whole new filter (bonus points if you can make the Polar Coordinates filter do something useful).

# ◆ Dynamic Effects with Motion Blur

Animation on Web pages usually requires a large file size, so if there's a way to suggest motion using a still image instead of a full-blown GIF animation, do it. We're going to add some dynamism to the *Stitch* name without moving it.

1.  Make sure black is the foreground color.

2.  Choose the Type tool and click near the top of the image (see Figure 5–8).

**FIGURE 5–8** The Type tool

3.  Choose a size of 40 points.

4.  Font: Trebuchet MS if you have it, Helvetica if you don't.

5.  Type the word "stitch."

6.  Click OK.

7.  Now we want to make the text italic to add a sense of motion. If you don't have the italic version of Trebuchet MS, go to Layer→Type→Render Type to transform the text layer into a regular layer.

8.  Make a copy of the layer.

9.  Go to Edit→Transform→Skew.

10. Skew the text slightly to the right by taking your cursor and dragging the top center point to the right (see Figure 5–9).

**FIGURE 5–9** Skewing text

11. Press Enter or double-click inside the rectangle to cement the change.

12. Make a copy of the skewed layer.

13. Go to Filters→Blur→Motion Blur.

14. Choose an angle of 0° and a distance of 20 pixels.

15. Save your work.

# ◆ Saving Time with Eliminate White

We want a picture of a woman lounging on a boat against our simple sea/sky background. The best image we could find was a studio shot of a woman on a boat against a white background. We somehow have to eliminate all the white in the image outside the woman and the boat, but keep the white in her dress. This process requires several steps, the first of which is using the Eliminate White filter.

Eliminate White is a nonPhotoshop filter but is often useful. Download it from http://www.adobe.com and place the plug-in in the Plug-ins folder in your Adobe Photoshop directory.

1. Once you've placed the Eliminate White in your Plug-ins folder and have restarted Photoshop, open the *Stitch* file and select the layer containing the image of the woman and the boat.

2. Make a copy of the layer and hide the original.

3. Make sure the default foreground and background colors are chosen (see Figure 5–10).

**FIGURE 5–10** Default foreground and background colors

4. Click on the black and white squares below the larger squares to get the default colors.

5. On the layer's copy, apply Filter→Transparency→Eliminate White.

6. The image will wash out more than you expect (or want). Choose Layer→Matting→Remove White Matte. This is an essential step in the Eliminate White process.

Looks great except that all the white in the woman's dress just disappeared and the whole thing is now slightly transparent (see Figure 5–11).

**FIGURE 5–11** The transparent woman and boat

To get around this, brush in white where you need it and merge the layer.

1. In the same image we've been working on, create a new layer and place it below the transparent woman layer.

2. Select the Brush tool and a medium-sized brush.

3. Paint white within the image. If you go over the edges, just erase the white.

4. Save your work.

Another way to achieve this effect would be to create a layer mask over the woman and then hide all of the white you don't want, but we've found the Eliminate White method to be faster.

## ◆ Useful Effects with Blur and Blending

The image of the woman and boat is a nice one, but it's a little too sharp and concrete for such an ethereal, atmospheric background.

We can fix this with a little blur and the Blending menu in the Layers palette (see Figure 5–12).

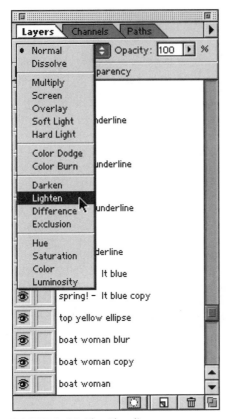

**FIGURE 5–12** The Blending menu

The blending menu determines how the appearance of a layer is affected by the layers below it, or how that layer blends with the others.

First, we'll need to combine the transparent woman and boat with the white underneath them.

1. Select the layer with the transparent woman.

2. Link the layer with the white behind the woman and boat (see Figure 5–13).

3. Go to Layer→Merge Linked. This combines all linked layers in the file into one layer.

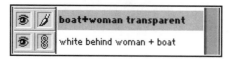

**FIGURE 5–13** The linked layers

4. Make a copy of the merged layer and select it.

5. Go to Filter→Blur→Gaussian Blur.

6. Enter a Blur Radius of 5 pixels.

7. Select Lighten from the Blending menu.

Effects with the Blending menu can produce some very subtle, professional touches to images. We suggest you experiment often with blending.

## Recap

We've scratched the surface of what's available in Photoshop as far as filters, blending, and general effects. You've learned how to create your own gradients, how to judiciously apply both weird and common filters, and how to use the Blending menu to affect a layer's appearance.

## Advanced Projects

Create the rest of the homepage on your own. We've covered most of the more complicated effects, but you should finish it up. We'll give you a hint on how to create the yellow elliptical ring, though.

1. Make a new layer.

2. Using the Marquee tool, draw an ellipse.

3. Choose the Paint Bucket and fill the ellipse with yellow.

4. Go to Select→Modify→Contract.

5. Contract the selection by 2 pixels.

6. Press the Delete key. Voilá! A ring.

# 6 The Art of the Cut

*Your homepage is just like the perfect cake—it only stays whole for a little while before it has to be sliced up and enjoyed by many people. In order for everyone to be able to view your creation quickly, you have to master the why, where, and how of cutting up your image.*

## ◆ Why You Need to Cut Up Your Image

Let's say you have an image that is approximately 600 pixels × 600 pixels such as the *Stitch* homepage (see Figure 6–1). The entire graphic is 560K in size and entirely too large to put up as is, even if we could. As you learned earlier, we will need to create a much more compressed version of this image. We'll either use a GIF, JPEG compression, or a combination of both. One of the ways to speed up the download of a page is to create many smaller images from the one big one. If you'd like to have individual buttons that do something fun like a *rollover*, you will need to make two images for each button. A rollover is what you see when your cursor is placed over a button on a Web page and something happens to it, like changing color or popping up (see Figure 6–2.). A rollover is created with some fancy scripting inside your HTML code called JavaScript. What the code actually tells the page to do when it sees a rollover is to replace the image that's there with another one. It's that simple. But in order to replace the image you have to have another one the exact same size. Guess how you do that? Yes, *guidelines*. If you want more details on Java-Script and rollovers, see the JavaScript book in this *Essential* series—*Essential JavaScript for Web Professionals*.

**FIGURE 6–1** Detail of the *Stitch* online fashion magazine homepage before we begin to cut it apart for a quick Web download

**FIGURE 6–2** Rollover is a term used to define a piece of JavaScript code that allows an image to change when a cursor is moved over it

## ◆ Preparing Your Image for the Cut

There are several ways to cut up your image using Photoshop. The best method is to use guidelines. As a reminder, guides live a secret and peaceful life in the ruler surrounding your image. They lend themselves out to designers to help make the day a little easier. If you don't see the ruler, go to the top menu bar and select View→Show Rulers. To create guides, first go to the top menu bar and select View→Show Guides. If you see Hide Guides that means you are already set up to use the guidelines.

While using any of the tools in the palette, bring your cursor to the ruler bar and the cursor will turn into a pointer (see Figure 6–3). Click and drag a guideline into your image. The guideline default color is blue. Unless you've change your defaults, that's what you'll see.

**FIGURE 6–3** Moving your cursor to the ruler bar will allow you to click and drag a guideline into your image

You can pull as many guidelines into your image as you need, as you'll see in a moment. First, you need to know where to move the guides.

## ◆ Where to Place the Guidelines

You'll need to separate your image into many little rectangles. It won't work to try and break them up into ovals or other inventive polygons. Think *grids*. Just a plain old x and y axis. Just like graph paper or a chessboard. You will be using the guidelines to separate elements such as buttons, categories, headers, and photos from solid areas. If we were to create the grid the way we are actually going to break up the *Stitch Magazine* page, we need to do one step first. Print out a copy of the homepage and then take a ruler and draw lines separating the areas you want (see Figure 6–4).

**FIGURE 6–4** The sections of the *Stitch* homepage as we want to break them apart

We have to pull the guidelines down from the ruler and block out all the little rectangles that we will need. More small sections are created than we actually need (see Figure 6–5). That's why it's best to refer to your original printout with the hand-drawn rules that show you the areas you will break apart.

**FIGURE 6–5** The page as it appears with all the guidelines in place

The next thing you need to do is copy the entire image and paste it in a new document. To copy the entire image, including all layers, hold down the Command key and press A (on a Mac), or hold down the Control key and press A (on a PC), to select all. Then hold down the Command and Shift keys and press C (on a Mac), or hold down the Control and Shift keys and press C (on a PC), to copy all layers at once. This allows all the layers to be blended into one layer. Good thing you saved your original to work on it as a flat image.

## ◆ Making the Cut

Once you've got the guidelines in place and a flat image, you can begin to cut up the image.

## Using Photoshop to Make the Cut

1. Click on the Rectangular Marquee tool.

2. Drag the marquee from the upper-left edge to the bottom right of the first area to be cut.

3. Select Edit→Copy.

4. Select File→New.

5. Click OK. Whatever you've just copied will determine the height and width of the new window.

6. Select Edit→Paste.

7. This gives you a new window with your cut piece in it.

8. Select Edit→Save and give the file a name with a .psd suffix.

9. This allows you the opportunity of trying different compression methods without going back to the main image.

10. Click OK.

11. Select a separate folder for your new images to avoid confusion.

12. Use a naming structure in plain wording so you will know where the pieces go.

13. Click OK.

14. Do this with each of the pieces of your image.

15. You can optimize the images later using one of the techniques mentioned in Chapter 3, "Making Images Web-Ready."

## Other Methods of Cutting

There are several different programs available for automatic cutting and slicing such as ImageReady (Adobe) Fireworks (Macromedia). These programs have some very distinct advantages and some disadvantages. While these products allow you to automatically slice an image along lines and then create an HTML page, they cut out every single rectangle that was created within the mass of guidelines. Using Photoshop and doing it rectangle by rectangle is our method of choice.

# ◆ GIF or JPEG Once Again

When you cut up your images you can choose the best method for each new piece. As we discussed in Chapter 3, you can break up your image into GIF or JPEG format. If you have solid color areas, a good choice would probably be GIF. If you have a photograph or a sky that has banding (crude color transitions that create many bands), such as the woman on the cover of *Stitch*, you might choose JPEG compression. Again, the best method is to try both and see what looks best when you put your images together.

# ◆ Compressing Your Files

Once your images are cut apart, you can optimize them in your favorite method from Chapter 3. Go back and review the details of each method of compression. There are advantages to creating GIFs and JPEGs in Photoshop and advantages to the other programs as well. The entire job can be completed perfectly using Photoshop.

### GIF Compression

1. Open the cut-up images you saved as .psd files.
2. For each image select File→Export→GIF89a Export.
3. Make sure each image has a maximum of 255 colors.
4. Click OK.
5. Give the files the same name with a .gif extension.

### JPEG Compression

1. Open the cut-up images you saved as .psd files.
2. For each image select File→Save As.
3. A new window will pop up asking you to name the file and pick a format.
4. Select JPEG from the pull-down menu.
5. Give the files the same name with a .jpg or .jpeg extension.
6. Click OK.

**7.** Another options palette will pop up asking you to pick the quality of the image from low to high.

**8.** Choose medium and click OK.

Now you are ready to put it all together or hand it off to the programmer.

## ◆ Putting It Together

Now you have a bunch of little images. What's next? This is where your HTML skills come in handy. There are so many ways to create an HTML page that we will not give you one exact method. We'll give you the code to create the *Stitch* online fashion magazine homepage. You'll need to give the images over to your programmer or do it yourself using  the JavaScript book mentioned earlier, as well as our *Essential CSS & DHTML for Web Professionals*.

```
<HTML>
<HEAD>

<TITLE>Stitch</TITLE>

</HEAD>
<BODY BGCOLOR="#FFFFFF">

<TABLE BORDER="0" CELLPADDING="0" CELLSPACING="0">
<TR>
    <TD COLSPAN="2"><IMG SRC="topdate.gif" ALT="Date"
    WIDTH="600" HEIGHT="23" BORDER="0"></TD>
</TR>
<TR>
    <TD COLSPAN="2"><IMG SRC="header.gif" ALT="Stitch
    Online Magazine" WIDTH="600" HEIGHT="136"
    BORDER="0"></TD>
</TR>
<TR>
    <TD COLSPAN="2"><IMG SRC="center.gif" WIDTH="477"
    HEIGHT="64" BORDER="0" ISMAP USEMAP="#helpers"></TD>
</TR>
<TR>
    <TD ROWSPAN="9" VALIGN="TOP">
<A HREF="dirt.html"><IMG SRC="dirt.gif" ALT="Dirt"
WIDTH="145" HEIGHT="27" BORDER="0"></A>
<BR>
```

```
<A HREF="money.html"><IMG SRC="money.gif" ALT="Money"
WIDTH="145" HEIGHT="26" BORDER="0"></A>
<BR>
<A HREF="trends.html"><IMG SRC="trends.gif" ALT="Trends"
WIDTH="145" HEIGHT="25" BORDER="0"></A>
<BR>
<A HREF="haute.html"><IMG SRC="haute.gif" ALT="Haute"
WIDTH="145" HEIGHT="25" BORDER="0"></A>
<BR>
<A HREF="street.html"><IMG SRC="street.gif" ALT="Street"
WIDTH="145" HEIGHT="28" BORDER="0"></A>
<BR>
<A HREF="profiles.html"><IMG SRC="profiles.gif"
ALT="Profiles" WIDTH="145" HEIGHT="28" BORDER="0"></A>
<BR>
<A HREF="column.html"><IMG SRC="column.gif"
ALT="Columns" WIDTH="145" HEIGHT="25" BORDER="0"></A>
<BR>
<A HREF="store.html"><IMG SRC="store.gif" ALT="Store"
WIDTH="145" HEIGHT="28" BORDER="0"></A>
<BR>
<IMG SRC="bottomleft.gif" WIDTH="145" HEIGHT="157"
BORDER="0"></TD><TD><IMG SRC="mainimage.gif" WIDTH="455"
HEIGHT="377" BORDER="0"></TD>
</TR>
</TABLE>

</BODY>
</HTML>
```

## RECAP

In this chapter you learned:

- Why you need to cut an image into smaller pieces.
- How to cut up an image by using guidelines.
- Where to cut the image for the most benefit.
- How to flatten your image.
- Advantages and disadvantages of using other programs to break up your image.
- When to optimize using GIF and JPEG methods.

## ADVANCED PROJECTS

1.  Go to some of your favorite Web pages and take a screen capture of the page. You can do this quickly by holding down the Command and Shift keys and pressing 3 (on a Mac), or holding down the Alt and Print Screen keys (on a PC), and then open a Photoshop document and paste in the image.

2.  Open that image in Photoshop.

3.  Print the image and draw the guidelines on the page so you can break it up.

4.  Create the guidelines on the image using the pull-down guides.

5.  Since the page will already be flat, cut up the images.

6.  Save as GIF and JPEG at your discretion and testing.

7.  Do this with several homepages to get the hang of it.

# 7 Advanced Photo Altering

## IN THIS CHAPTER

- Advanced Rubber Stamp Tool
- Creating Duotones: Adding Color to Black-and-White Images
- Hue and Saturation
- Color Balance
- Changing Background Images
- Using Levels
- Cleaning Up Previously Printed Materials
- Recap
- Advanced Projects

## ◆ Advanced Rubber Stamp Tool

Now that you've mastered using the Rubber Stamp tool to remove skin blemishes from photos, we're going to show you a few more applications for this useful tool. You'll learn how to eliminate scratches from images, remove glare from eyeglasses, get rid of red "devil" eyes, and fix old photos to make them useful.

### Scratched Negatives or Images

Every photo that lands on your desk to be put up on the Web will not be perfect. One of the many image problems you'll face is the scratched negative or scan (see Figure 7–1). The boss wants a particular photo for the homepage of *Stitch Magazine*. Of the hundreds of photographs available, the Boss has to pick the one with a scratch right through the model's face and body. Of course, you are expected to "do your Photoshop magic" on the image. Here's how you will save the day and the homepage.

**FIGURE 7–1** The original image with a scratch on the negative visible on the scanned image

1. Make a copy of the image first so you can go back to the original if you aren't satisfied with your results the first time around.

2. Zoom in on the image so it's as large as it can be and still recognizable (see Figure 7–2).

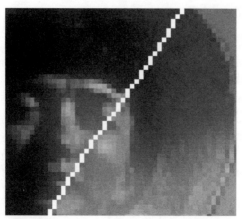

**FIGURE 7–2** The enlarged original image allows you to see details

3. Select the Rubber Stamp tool (see Figure 7–3).

**FIGURE 7–3** The Rubber Stamp tool

4. Make sure the Rubber Stamp Options palette is set to Normal, 100% opacity, and Aligned (see Figure 7–4).

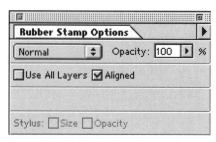

**FIGURE 7–4** The Rubber Stamp Options palette

5. Select the smallest brush available (see Figure 7–5).

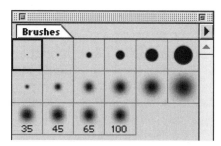

**FIGURE 7–5** Selecting the smallest brush from the Brushes palette

6. Look at the image with the scratch and determine which pixel color should fill in the scratched gap. Is it a pixel to the left, right, top, or bottom of the scratch?

7. Place the Rubber Stamp tool on the pixel that has the same color you want to use to fill in the gap.

8. Press the Option key and click to pick up the color you want to use to fill in the scratch.

9. Place the Rubber Stamp tool over the gap and click once.

10. This action takes the color you picked up and places it right in the gap.

11. Continue these steps until the gap has been filled in (see Figure 7–6).

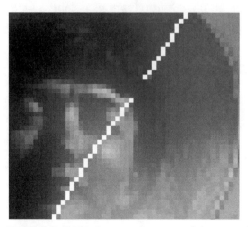

**FIGURE 7–6** The image after part of the scratch has been removed

## Removing Glare from Eyeglasses

You've done wonders so far for images placed on the Web and word of your Photoshop prowess has gotten around the office. So, you aren't surprised when the boss comes to you and hands you a photo of the CFO and you see bright white spots on his glasses (see Figure 7–7). After the obligatory questions about having the photo reshot, the boss tells you it's not possible and to do the best you can.

This one is not as easy to fix as the scratched negative. This requires some finessing with the Rubber Stamp tool.

1. Start with a copy of the original art.

2. Zoom in on the image so it's as large as it can be and still recognizable (see Figure 7–8).

3. Select the Rubber Stamp tool (see Figure 7–3).

4. Make sure the Rubber Stamp tool Options box is set to Normal, 100% opacity, and Aligned (see Figure 7–4).

FIGURE 7–7 Image of the CFO with a glare on his glasses

FIGURE 7–8 Enlarged image of the lens glare

5. Select the smallest brush available (see Figure 7–5).

6. Look at the image with the lens glare and determine which pixel color should fill in the glare. Is it a pixel to the left, right, top, or bottom of the glare?

7. Place the Rubber Stamp tool on the pixel that has the same color you want to use to fill in the glare.

8. Press the Option key and click to pick up the color you want to use to fill in the glare.

9. Place the Rubber Stamp tool over the glare and click once.

10. This action takes the color you picked up and places it over the glare.

11. Continue these steps until the glare has been filled in (see Figure 7–9).

12. You may need to start over with the Smudge tool and/or use a "fuzzier" brush if you are not satisfied with your results. Remember to always work with a copy of the original.

**FIGURE 7–9** Image of the CFO without the glare on his eyeglasses

## Removing "Red Eye"

You've just been handed a stack of photos taken from the *Stitch Magazine* launch party and you've been asked to put them up on the Web under the Paparazzi section. The only trouble is, the world's greatest living designer, Jean LeFaux, has red eyes in the photograph (see Figure 7–10). Your task is to take away Jean's "evil eye." This is one of the more difficult procedures, and it may feel like you are performing reconstructive eye surgery. So put away the caffeinated drinks and let's get started. This can also be done using the Hue/Saturation/Color palette (see Hue, Saturation, and Color later in this chapter).

1. Start with a copy of the original art.

2. Zoom in on the image so it's as large as it can be and still recognizable.

3. Select the Rubber Stamp tool (see Figure 7–3).

4. Make sure the Rubber Stamp tool option box is set to Normal, 100% opacity, and Aligned (see Figure 7–4).

5. Select the smallest brush available (see Figure 7–5).

6. Look at the red eye and determine what the color of the eye is, if possible. Determine the area that should be color and the area that should be the black of the pupil.

**FIGURE 7–10** Image of the famous designer Jean LeFaux suffering snapshot-camera "red eye"

7. Often, the photo is small and it's going to be just a matter of taking out the red and replacing it with a dark color.

8. Even if Jean's eyes are light blue, in snapshot-camera photos, eye color almost never shows up at a distance. It's usually just a dark area without distinction between the pupil and the colored iris.

9. Place the Rubber Stamp tool on the pixel that has the same color you want to fill in the gap. If you can't see the color, use a dark color that is near the red.

10. Press the Option key and click to pick up the color you want to use to fill in the red eye.

11. Place the Rubber Stamp tool over the eye and click once.

12. This action takes the color you picked up and places it right in the eye.

13. Continue these steps until the red eye has been effectively removed (see Figure 7–11).

14. Remember to always work with a copy of the original.

FIGURE 7–11 Image of designer Jean LeFaux with the "red eye" removed

## Updating Old Photos

Just when you thought you'd had enough visits from people wanting miracles, the head of human resources drops by your cube with praise for your work. As you suspected, even HR wants something from you. After you bargain for an extra comp day, you ask what is needed. It turns out that the new CFO, Bobby Bookcooker, wants a different photo up on the Web. The problem is that Bobby has a lapel pin from his old company on his shirt collar (see Figure 7–12). You're in luck. This is the classic situation for using the Rubber Stamp tool.

1. Start with a copy of the original art.

2. Zoom in on the lapel so it's as large as it can be while you can still recognize the pattern of the material.

3. Select the Rubber Stamp tool (see Figure 7–3).

4. Make sure the Rubber Stamp tool option box is set to Normal, 100% opacity, and Aligned (see Figure 7–4).

5. There might be a solid-color lapel or a pattern.

6. If it's a pattern, select a brush that has sharp edges (see Figure 7–13).

**FIGURE 7–12** CFO Bobby Bookcooker's errant lapel pin

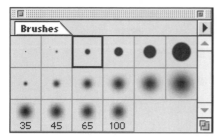

**FIGURE 7–13** Selecting a sharp-edged brush from the Brushes palette

7.  If the lapel is a solid color, pick a fuzzy-edged brush (see Figure 7–14).

8.  Place the Rubber Stamp tool on the pixel next to the lapel pin.

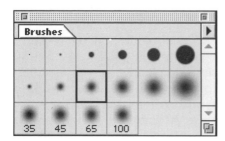

**FIGURE 7–14** Selecting a fuzzy-edged brush from the Brushes palette

9. Press the Option key and click to pick up the lapel color next to the pin.

10. Place the Rubber Stamp tool over the gap and click once.

11. This action takes the color you picked up and places it over the lapel pin and effectively removes the pin.

12. Continue these steps until the lapel pin has been covered (see Figure 7–15).

FIGURE 7–15 CFO Bobby Bookcooker's new lapel, sans pin

13. Remember to always work with a copy of the original.

## ◆ Creating Duotones: Adding Color to Black-and-White Images

Just as the day was beginning to shape up, the director of marketing comes in and very loudly exclaims, "After my wife left her Faux Furniture Finishing class at the adult education center last night, she stepped into the beginning desktop publishing class. She told me you should never mix black-and-white and color photographs. So I want you to go into the photo gallery section and either take out all the black-and-white photos or do something else with them."

Never one to doubt the information gleaned from such valued sources, you set about figuring out how to add some color where there is none. This is a simple process: You are going to create a *duotone*. A duotone is just what it sounds like—two tones. Same with the tritone and quadtone, which are all accomplished through the same process.

1. Open up a black-and-white photo (see Figure 7–16).

**FIGURE 7–16** A black-and-white photo that requires some color

2. In the top menu bar, select Image→Mode→Grayscale.

3. Only 8-bit grayscale images can be converted to duotone, tritone, or quadtone.

4. In the top menu bar, select Image→Mode→Duotone.

5. A Duotone dialog box will appear on your screen (see Figure 7–17).

6. Make sure Preview is checked so you can see how your image is progressing.

7. The Type box in the dialog box should say "Duotone." The options of monotone, tritone, and quadtone are also selected when needed.

8. The next items listed are Inks, which refer to the colors you will be using. Since you've chosen a black-and-white photo, the only ink selected will be black.

9. Ink 2 will have a white box below the black Ink 1 box.

10. Inks 3 and 4 should be grayed out. If not, make sure you have Duotone selected in the Type box.

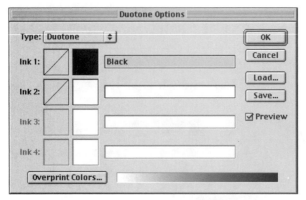

**FIGURE 7–17** The Duotone Options dialog box

**11.** Click on the white box next to Ink 2, not the first box with the diagonal line.

**12.** A Color Picker dialog box will appear (see Figure 7–18).

**13.** Pick your second color from this box. A duotone can be any two colors, but for this exercise we'll use black as the first color.

**14.** In the Color Picker dialog box, you will see that the first large square area has color gradients of one color, a vertical bar of many colors, and some buttons on the right.

**15.** Below the OK and Cancel buttons, there is a button labeled either Picker or Custom (see Figure 7–18).

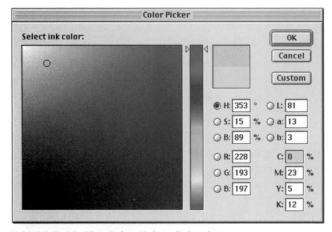

**FIGURE 7–18** The Color Picker dialog box

**16.** If you are in the Color Picker area, the box will give you the option of going to Custom colors, and vice versa.

**17.** For this exercise, make sure the button says "Custom" so you know you're in the Color Picker area.

**18.** To choose a color to work with, use your cursor to move the triangle markers on the vertical color-gradated bar (see Figure 7–19). Pick any color.

**FIGURE 7–19** The vertical color-gradated bar in the Color Picker dialog box

**19.** Now it's time to determine how saturated or rich you want the second color to be.

**20.** When your cursor moves into the single color-gradated box, it turns into a hollow circle.

**21.** Click your cursor in the upper right-hand corner of the box (see Figure 7–20). This will give you a 100% color to work with.

**FIGURE 7–20** Selecting a color in the Color Picker

**22.** For now, ignore all the numbers below the OK button.

**23.** You will now be back at the Duotone dialog box and a second color will have been added to the Ink 2 area (see Figure 7–21).

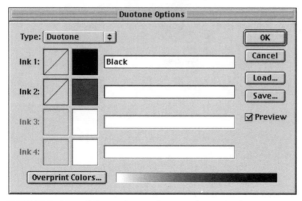

**FIGURE 7–21** Adding Ink or color number 2 in the Duotone Options dialog box

**24.** You will also see that the photograph now has a tint of the color you chose.

**25.** In order to manipulate how much black and how much Ink 2 to use, click on the first Ink 1 square with the diagonal line (see Figure 7–22).

**FIGURE 7–22** Clicking on the Ink 1 square with the diagonal line to determine the amount of a color

**26.** This brings up the Duotone Curve box. This allows you to raise or lower the level of color used. In this case, we'll reduce the amount of black (see Figure 7–23).

**27.** With your cursor, click on the diagonal line in the middle and pull it down so there is a curve in the line (see Figure 7–24).

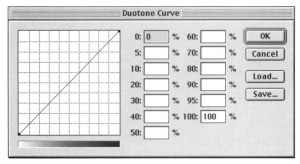

**FIGURE 7–23** The Duotone Curve slider lets you use either the curve bar or the numerical values to change the color

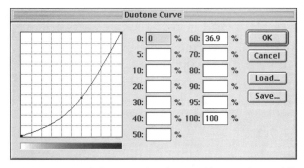

**FIGURE 7–24** Clicking on the diagonal line in the middle and pulling it down so there is a curve in the line

**28.** You'll notice that your photograph has less black in it and more of the Ink 2 color.

**29.** Just keep playing with the curves until you find a color balance that looks nice to you.

**30.** Again, remember that PCs see images a little darker than Macs. Therefore, if you are on a Mac, make the image a little lighter than you think it should be, since 85% of your viewers will be on a PC.

**31.** In order to recreate the same duotone for all your black-and-white images, make sure you write down the names of your ink colors and the curve numbers. If you do all the images one after another, Photoshop will keep the duotone settings you last used in order to create many duotones quickly.

# ◆ Hue and Saturation

As you are piecing together the last sections of the *Stitch Magazine* Web site, the creative director calls you over to the light table. You both decide that it would be a great idea to show a dress in all the colors in which it's sold, but the same pose isn't available in each color. You also have created several icon buttons for the site and the colors need to change. The last thing you want to do is recreate everything. There's one tool that will allow you to do both: Hue and Saturation. As we mentioned earlier, this is also a great tool to use to get the red eye out of photographs.

The Hue/Saturation dialog box allows you to adjust the color, the saturation (purity) of the color, and its lightness.

## *Changing Dress Colors*

You have one pose for a dress and you'd like to show it in six more colors. Here's how to do it.

1.  Make a copy of the original image of the dress and work on the copy.

2.  Use the Lasso tool to select the area of the dress you'd like to change (see Figure 7–25).

**FIGURE 7–25** Selecting the area of the dress to change its color

3. In the top menu bar, select Image→Adjust→Hue/Saturation.

4. The Hue/Saturation dialog box will appear (see Figure 7–26).

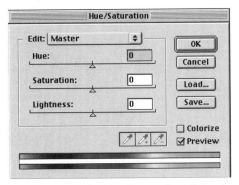

**FIGURE 7–26** The Hue/Saturation dialog box

5. Click on the Colorize check box (see Figure 7–27).

**FIGURE 7–27** Clicking the Colorize check box in the Hue/Saturation dialog box

6. Adjust the first and second sliders of Hue and Saturation until you have the desired color.

7. Save your work and create a new layer with the same area selected. Then, all you have to do is select Hue/Saturation and slide the colors around.

## Changing Icon Button Colors

Let's say you have a great button that you created using layer effects and inner bevel (see Figure 7–28). If you need to change the color of the button to create a different color button for each section, use Hue/Saturation again.

**FIGURE 7–28** Your cool icon with inner bevel layer effects

1. Start with a copy of your cool icon button.

2. Make sure you click the layer on which the icon resides.

3. In the top menu bar, select Image→Adjust→Hue/Saturation.

4. Use the sliders to change colors.

5. Use Colorize if you can't find a color combination you like.

6. If Preview is selected you will be able to see the changes.

7. Before you click OK, write down the numbers of the three settings in case you have to modify several icons. Once you click OK, the settings for Hue/Saturation become ground zero for the new image and all the sliders read 0.

8. Create a new layer for each color button.

9. Name your layers for their sections or colors so you will recognize them when you need to use them.

### Getting the Red Eye Out—Part II

As we mentioned earlier, using Hue/Saturation is another great way to get rid of red eye. It may also be faster and easier.

1. Open the image with the red eyes (see Figure 7–10). Make a copy and work on it.

2. Zoom in on the image until the size of the eye is easy to work on.

3. Use the Lasso tool to select the red portion of the eye.

4. In the top menu bar, select Image→Adjust→Hue/Saturation.

5. Use the sliders to change the Hue and Saturation.

6. Click the Colorize button if needed.

## ◆ Color Balance

### Changing Facial Tones

As you look over the images for the Web site, you notice that some of the models' faces are too yellow. To adjust the color, you will be using a tool similar to Hue/Saturation: Color Balance.

1. Open the image of a model's face.

2. Using the Lasso tool, select the model's face.

3. In the top menu bar, select Image→Adjust→Color Balance (see Figure 7–29).

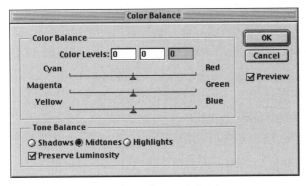

**FIGURE 7–29** The Color Balance dialog box

4. Hide the selection by selecting View→Hide Edges in the top menu bar.

5. You still have a selection, but it won't interfere with how you see the edges.

6. Use the sliders to move away from the color you don't want.

7. If there is too much yellow, slide the slider away from the yellow and toward blue.

8. Try many options until you get it right.

9. Before you click OK, write down the numbers you used to create the new facial tone and use them as a basis for the next yellowish face.

## ◆ Changing Background Images

So far you've fixed red eyes, eyeglass glare, errant lapel pins, facial tones, and blemishes. You get back to your desk and see the following Post-It note from the copy editor: "You have 10 photographs of

the management team and there are several different backdrops."
Now you need to make them all the same. You decide to create a
new backdrop and put it in all the photographs.

If you have access to any stock photography books, take a
look and see if they have a textured piece of art that will work for
your background needs. It may be worth the nominal fee you pay
for the right to use the texture. If you find one, great; if not, create
a new one.

There are several ways to create backgrounds that mimic a
photographer's studio backdrops. We'll show you two here.

1. Open a new blank image. Make it 4 inches × 4 inches so it
   will be larger than any photograph you have.

2. Select a dark blue from your palette.

3. Fill the blank with the blue you selected.

4. In the top menu bar, select Filter→Artistic→Film Grain
   (see Figure 7–30).

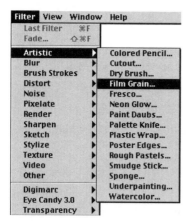

**FIGURE 7–30** Selecting the Film Grain filter

5. The Film Grain dialog box will appear (see Figure 7–31).

6. Move the top slider to the far right, creating the most film
   grain available.

7. Click OK.

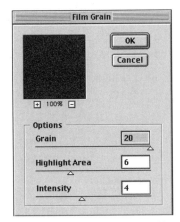

**FIGURE 7–31** Selecting the filter settings for Film Grain

> **8.** In the top menu bar, select Filter→Blur→Gaussian Blur (see Figure 7–32).

**FIGURE 7–32** Creating a Gaussian Blur on the existing Film Grain

> **9.** Make sure Preview is checked so you can see what it looks like as you experiment.
>
> **10.** Move the slider to 3.0 pixels.
>
> **11.** Click OK.
>
> **12.** Now you have one background to use.

To create another type of background simulating the photographer's studio backdrop, let's try some clouds. With a gradated image like clouds, you will probably need to make the image a JPEG when you put it on the Web.

1.  Open a new blank image. Make it 4 inches × 4 inches so it will be larger than any photograph you have.

2.  Select a dark blue from your palette.

3.  Fill the blank with the blue you selected.

4.  In the top menu bar, select Filter→Render→Clouds (see Figure 7–33).

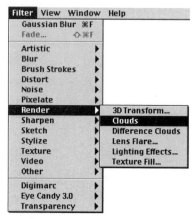

**FIGURE 7–33** Selecting the Render/Clouds filter

5.  A new background with clouds will appear (see Figure 7–34).

**FIGURE 7–34** The new background with clouds rendered

6.  Now you have another background to use.

Once you have a background or two that you'd like to use on all the photographs, proceed with the next steps.

1.  Open the first of the management team photographs.

2. Click on the New Layer icon at the bottom of the Layers palette (see Figure 7–35).

**FIGURE 7–35** The new layer icon at the bottom of the Layers palette

3. In the Layers palette there will be two layers: "Layer 1" and "Background" (see Figure 7–36).

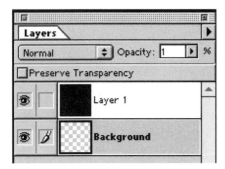

**FIGURE 7–36** Layer 1 and the Background layer

4. Double-click on the Background layer and name it Layer 0. It will be the default when double-clicked (see Figure 7–37).

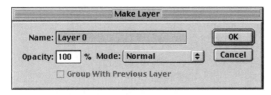

**FIGURE 7–37** Rename Background to Layer 0

5. You need to do this in order to move a layer below the Background layer.

6. With your cursor, drag Layer 1 below Layer 0 (see Figure 7–38).

7. Now select the layer with the photograph on it.

8. Zoom in on the image so you can see the details near the body you will be removing.

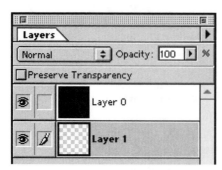

**FIGURE 7–38** Drag Layer 1 below Layer 0

9.   Using your Magic Wand or Lasso tool, select the background.

10.   Delete the background.

11.   You should see the photograph and a lightly colored checkerboard pattern behind it. That is the transparency behind the image.

12.   Now open one of the backgrounds you created.

13.   Copy it and paste it into the image with the photograph or just drag the Background layer from the Layers palette into the photograph.

14.   In the Layers palette, use your cursor to drag the background to the layer between Layer 1 and Layer 0.

15.   You will see the new background behind the photograph.

16.   With the new background image layer selected, use your Move tool to maneuver the background so that it fits your aesthetics.

17.   Look for edges near hair and skin to make sure you removed enough of the old background.

## ◆ Using Levels

You are looking through the archives of the magazine covers and you notice that they have all scanned a little cream-colored instead of bright white, and that the blacks have all turned a little gray. This is where the ability to manipulate levels comes in handy.

**1.** Open the first magazine image (see Figure 7–39).

**FIGURE 7–39** Printed *Stitch Magazine* cover with dull whites and blacks

**2.** In the top menu bar, select Image→Adjust→Levels (see Figure 7–40).

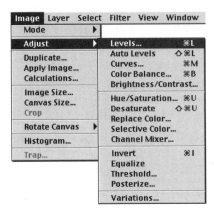

**FIGURE 7–40** Selecting Levels from the top menu bar

3. You will see a box with lines that look like levels on a stereo tuner (see Figure 7–41).

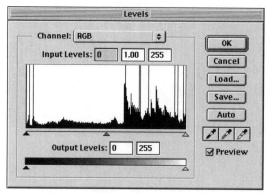

**FIGURE 7–41** The Levels dialog box

4. Make sure Preview is checked so you can see your progress.

5. To increase the blackness of the black, slide the triangle on the far left-hand side of the levels to the right and watch what the image does (see Figure 7–42). Stop when the darks reach the level you want.

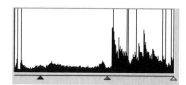

**FIGURE 7–42** Using the triangle slider to create blacker blacks

6. To increase the whiteness of the white, slide the triangle on the far right-hand side of the levels to the left and watch what the image does (see Figure 7–43). Stop when the whites reach the level you want.

7. You can also play with the midtones by sliding the center triangle.

8. Once you've got the white/black range that you want, open the rest of the images and find the right range for each image.

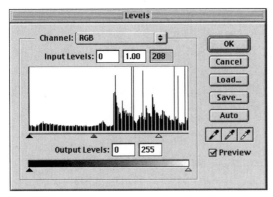

**FIGURE 7–43** Using the triangle slider to create whiter whites

# ◆ Cleaning Up Previously Printed Materials

The members of the archiving department stop by with your boss and together they decide that all the magazine advertisements ever created should be on the Web. However, you don't have all the electronic files that created the ads. You do have the existing advertisements that have been printed in other magazines.

The problem is that when an image is printed, it's made up of thousands of little colored dots; most often, cyan, magenta, yellow, and black. There may be some extra colors in there as well. When you scan previously printed material, you get what's called a *moiré pattern*. The little rosettes that make up the colors on the printed page are invisible to the eye from a proper reading distance; however, when scanned, all you see is those little patterns. There are a couple of ways to get rid of the moiré.

## Using Despeckle to Clean Up Images

1. Open a previously scanned image.

2. Look at the rosette dot patterns (see Figure 7–44).

3. In the top menu bar, select Filter→Noise→Despeckle (see Figure 7–45).

4. The Despeckle filter is applied and should eliminate some of the rosette pattern.

5. If you aren't satisfied with the results, try using the Median option discussed next.

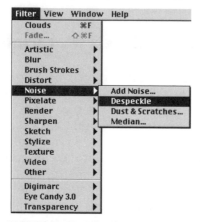

**FIGURE 7–44** Rosette patterns on a previously printed advertisement

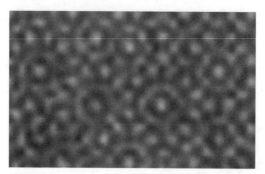

**FIGURE 7–45** Selecting Despeckle from the top menu bar

## Using Median to Clean Up Images

1. Open a previously scanned image.

2. Look at the rosette dot patterns (see Figure 7–44).

3. In the top menu bar, select Filter→Noise→Median (see Figure 7–46).

4. The Median dialog box will appear (see Figure 7–47).

5. It usually doesn't take more than a setting of 1 to get rid of the pattern.

6. If you aren't satisfied with the results, try using the Blur/ Sharpen method, discussed next.

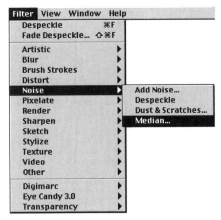

**FIGURE 7–46** Selecting Median from the top menu bar

**FIGURE 7–47** The Median dialog box

## Using Blur/Sharpen to Clean Up Images

1. Open a previously scanned image.

2. Look at the rosette dot patterns (see Figure 7–44).

3. In the top menu bar, select Filter→Blur→Gaussian Blur (see Figure 7–48).

4. The Gaussian Blur dialog box will appear (see Figure 7–49).

5. Select a radius number that will get rid of the rosette pattern.

6. Once the pattern is gone, with the same image selected, go to the top menu bar and select Filter→Sharpen→Unsharp Mask (see Figure 7–50).

7. Select a percentage amount that will give you the sharpness back without the rosettes.

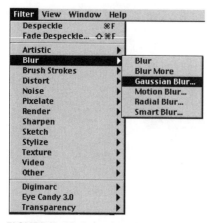

**FIGURE 7–48** Selecting Gaussian Blur from the top menu bar

**FIGURE 7–49** The Gaussian Blur dialog box

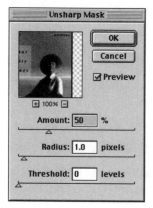

**FIGURE 7–50** The Unsharp Mask dialog box

## RECAP

Now you have the ability to do almost anything that comes across your desk in a real-world situation.

In this chapter you learned how to:

- Use the Rubber Stamp tool with more expertise: fix photos with scratches, remove glare from eyeglasses, eliminate "red eye," and remove items such as a lapel pin from clothing.
- Create duotones to bring some color to black-and-white photographs.
- Use Hue and Saturation to alter clothing color, button color, and as another alternative to getting rid of "red eye."
- Change skin tones using Color Balance.
- Create and change backgrounds on photos.
- Make the black and white parts of your images darker and lighter, respectively.
- Fix previously printed magazine images.

## ADVANCED PROJECTS

Here are some exercises to help you practice your new skills:

1. Find some scratched old photos and scan them, or create your own by drawing a line through existing digital images. Practice removing the scratch with the Rubber Stamp tool.

2. Find a picture in your family album of someone with glare on his or her glasses. Scan the image and practice removing the glare using the techniques you learned.

3. Dig into your family album again and scan some "red eye" photos. Practice taking out the red eye. Use either the Rubber Stamp tool or the Hue/Saturation dialog box.

4. If no "red eye" photos exist, try changing the color of people's eyes in photos. If you have a color printer, print them out and send them to people and see if they notice.

5. Find pictures of people with buttons on their shirts or suit jackets. Scan in those images and practice removing the buttons digitally.

6. Find any images on the Web or in photo albums or image libraries. Convert them to grayscale images and practice making duotones, tritones, and quadtones.

7. Find a landscape image and make a quadtone using four variations of gray from light to dark. Save a copy so you can see the difference between the two.

8. Find images of people from image disks or on the Web and practice changing their shirt and shoe colors.

9. Create a fancy icon button and make six different versions of it by changing the Hue and Saturation. Try doing it all in one document using layers.

10. Use some of the same images you have of people's faces and change their skin tones using Hue/Saturation.

11. Take four different head-shot photos from the Web or from image libraries and create new backgrounds for them. Make it appear as if they were all photographed on the same day in the same studio.

12. Find some "muddy" images and use Levels to brighten the whites and darken the blacks.

13. Scan many photos, from the newspaper to high-quality glossy magazines. Practice removing the moiré patterns with the Despeckle, Median, or Blur/Sharpen technique.

# 8 Tips and Tricks

## IN THIS CHAPTER

- Using Lower-Resolution Images
- Image Sizing in HTML
- Defining Patterns
- Checking Your Work
- Recap
- Advanced Projects
- Go Forth and Prosper

*We've taken you through many Photoshop Web essentials that we've encountered in the daily process of creating Web sites. We've talked about using Photoshop and have briefly mentioned other applications. All Web images are placed on the Web by use of an HTML page. So far, we've assumed either you, or someone else, knows how to put your images into an HTML page. Only a few references to HTML code have been used so far. In this chapter, we will give you the code for some tips and tricks. If you are not familiar with HTML, don't let it scare you—just give the images you create to your HTML programmer and explain what you want the final output to be. If you do know HTML, great—just add the code that is provided here and see what happens. There are many great HTML references online as well as in the bookstore if you are interested in learning. Now, let's move on to some fun miscellaneous info, tips, and tricks.*

# ◆ Using Lower-Resolution Images

### The Low Source Trick

This is a tip that is not used much anymore because image optimization has become such a fine art. Remember, the goal is to create very tightly optimized graphics for fast loading. This is strictly an artistic trick at this point in the Web's development. The technique calls for the designer to create two images. The first image is the one you want the viewer to see, and the second is a *low source* image. The latter can be a black-and-white image and can also be a very grainy representation of the image that is about to load. It can also be a different image.

An easy way to create a low source image is to take the image that will be the final loading image and alter it.

1.  Open the original image (see Figure 8–1).

FIGURE 8–1 Open the original image

**2.** Export the original to GIF format.

**3.** Save the original image as a new image and add "_small" to its filename (see Figure 8–2).

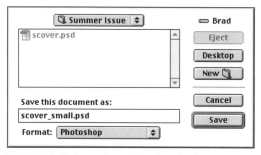

**FIGURE 8–2** Save the original with the name extension "_small"

**4.** In the top menu bar, select Image→Mode→Grayscale (see Figure 8–3).

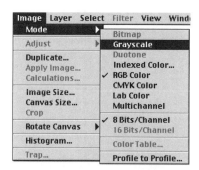

**FIGURE 8–3** Select Grayscale to convert the image to black and white

**5.** This will create a black-and-white version of your color art.

**6.** In the top menu bar, select Image→Mode→Bitmap.

**7.** You will have the option of resolution and pattern.

**8.** Use a resolution of 72 and start with a Diffusion pattern (see Figure 8–4). (If the resolution is less than 72 it will shrink the size of your graphic. The final effect is not as nice-looking that way.)

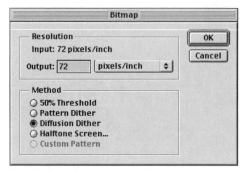

**FIGURE 8–4** Setting the Diffusion pattern for Bitmap mode

> **9.** Click OK and see the pattern it applies to your art (see Figure 8–5).

**FIGURE 8–5** The image with Diffusion applied

> **10.** If you want to try others, select Undo in the top menu bar and try again.

**11.** Once you have the pattern you like, in the top menu bar, select Image→Mode→Grayscale.

**12.** Select a ratio of 1 when prompted (see Figure 8–6).

**FIGURE 8–6** Using the Ratio palette to choose 1 for the conversion back to grayscale

**13.** In the top menu bar, select Image→Mode→RGB.

**14.** This allows you to export to a GIF format.

**15.** Export the graphic to GIF format.

**16.** Note the file size difference. It's approximately one quarter the size of the original.

Now that you've created the two pieces of art needed, you will need to add a little text to the HTML code to complete the effect. Here is the HTML code to display the original graphic:

```
<IMG SRC="sumcover.gif">
```

The only change you'll need to make to the code is to insert LOWSRC="filename_small.gif" between the IMG SRC tag, as shown in the following code. We've removed all the HEIGHT, WIDTH, ALT, and BORDER tags so you can see the difference.

```
<IMG LOWSRC="sumcover_small.gif" SRC=" sumcover.gif">
```

The final effect is to test the page in a browser. When the page loads, the first image that appears will be the grainy black-and-white art and then, magically, the color will fill in.

## The Low-Resolution Thumbnail Trick

The very same trick can be used for a page that has many *thumbnails* that need to load. On the Web, thumbnails are the small images that can be clicked to see the image in a large size (see next paragraph). At the online fashion magazine, *Stitch*, we may have an issue in which we need to show many photographs from the Fall show in Milan. Many images on a page, however small, often take forever to load.

Our viewers might be clicking quickly back and forth between the thumbnails and larger pictures. Use the low source trick for each thumbnail. Be warned that when you load two pictures, however small, you are putting a greater demand on the Web server. As we said earlier, it's a trick and is not to be used on every page.

### Small Image Clicks to a Larger Image

In order to make a small image clickable to a larger image, the code is almost the same as a standard link. A standard link tag directs the viewer to another HTML page.

```
<A HREF="page.html"><IMG SRC="scover_small.gif"></A>
```

The following code directs the viewer to another image. In this case, it's the same image, only larger. The difference in the code is the `"scover.gif"` that follows `<A HREF=`.

```
<A HREF="scover.gif"><IMG SRC="scover_small.gif"></A>
```

The action of the page is that when a small image is clicked, it tells the browser to get and display the larger image on its own page in the upper left on the default background.

If you want more control of how the larger image is displayed, an HTML page can be created with just the larger graphic on it. The image can be placed anywhere on the page with any background or caption.

## ◆ Image Sizing in HTML

We've been talking about creating different sizes of the same image for use on the Web. The most efficient use of a graphic is to create it at each size you will need. There are one or two instances in which you might want to use the same graphic and just size it up or down with the code. In HTML, the standard image source tag looks like this:

```
<IMG SRC="scover.gif" WIDTH="300" HEIGHT="200">
```

The HTML tells the browser what image to get and at what width and height to display it. (The BORDER and ALT tags have been left out for simplicity.) You can change the WIDTH and HEIGHT tags to make the image a percentage of its size or an odd-shaped image if you are after that effect. This is what WYSIWYG (What You See Is What You Get) HTML page creators do when they are sizing an image. This takes much longer for the server to load because it's still loading the original image and then sizing it. If you have the ability to create a smaller image, do so.

You might find yourself in a situation where you are handed a 10-year-old logo from another company. The marketing person may have no idea who actually created it. It might be the type of graphic that breaks up, loses colors, and looks bad every time you try to reduce its size in Photoshop. One way to get around this problem is to size the image using HTML.

In the previous example of HTML, which shows WIDTH and HEIGHT, we can make the image half its size by changing the WIDTH to 150 and the HEIGHT to 100. That will still not display very well, but it may be your only solution.

```
<IMG SRC="scover.gif" WIDTH="150" HEIGHT="100">
```

Be aware that when using HTML page creators, you may need to create several sizes for each image you want.

The reverse of scaling down with HTML is to enlarge doing the same thing. In this version, however, you will use this trick to enlarge a graphic so much that it becomes a large bitmapped piece of art.

1. Open a small image that is approximately 72 pixels × 72 pixels.

2. Export the image as a GIF.

3. Place the image on an HTML page by using the IMG SRC tag shown earlier.

4. Use 400 pixels × 400 pixels.

5. Test the page in an HTML browser. You will see a piece of art that no longer resembles the sharp lines that you had at 72 pixels × 72 pixels square. You will have an image that is jagged and bitmapped. This could be a nice graphic element for your page.

## ◆ Defining Patterns

### Creating Repeating Background Patterns

A background image does just that: It sits in the background as your other images load over it. Background images are *tiled*, which means that whatever you put in as an image will repeat itself across the page. A background image can be used to create a watermark, add some color and shape, or create a solid shape of color on a navigation bar. If you use a small image, it will repeat (see Figure 8–7). By using this technique, the browser only looks at one tile and then repeats it as many times as is necessary to fill the page. It only downloads one small file, saving download time.

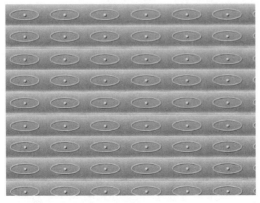

**FIGURE 8–7** Background images repeat across the page without special considerations

In order to create something that doesn't appear to repeat, you need to take a few extra steps. You need to create an image big enough for most browser resolutions, including the very large 1280 pixels × 1024 pixels. If you want a vertical bar of color on the navigation bar you need to do the following steps (see Figure 8–8).

**FIGURE 8–8** Create a vertical navigation bar that looks like this

1. Create a new document that is 1280 pixels × 25 pixels with a background of white.

2. Select your Rectangular Marquee tool and draw a 175-pixel rectangle starting at the upper-left part of the image.

3. Select a color from the Web Safe 216 color palette.

4. Select Edit→Fill and fill with foreground color.

5. You will have a small piece of the whole background image.

6. Select File→Export→GIF89a Export.

7. Name it background.gif.

8. Click OK to save.

9. Now you are ready to see what it looks like.

## How to Test Your Background Image

Again, you will need to ask your HTML programmer for help, or just check the image yourself by following these steps:

1. Create a new HTML page with the following code:

```
<HTML>
<HEAD>
<TITLE>Test My Background Page</TITLE>
</HEAD>
<BODY BGCOLOR="#FFFFFF" BACKGROUND="background.gif">
</BODY>
</HTML>
```

2. Make sure the background image is in the same folder as the HTML page.

3. Save the HTML page as b ʳ ʳroundtest.html.

4. Open the image in your browser from within the browser, or just drop the file onto the open browser window.

Now that you know how to make a background image, you can get creative. Test your new creations or have someone help you create the pages to show your backgrounds.

We've briefly talked about patterns for backgrounds. So far, we've talked about creating a solid background that repeats. Let's say you are in need of something a little more exotic than a solid color tile.

## Using Existing Patterns

Photoshop comes with 21 fantastic patterns, from arrowheads to wrinkles (see Figure 8–9). Each pattern is approximately 1-inch square to facilitate easy repeating.

**FIGURE 8–9** All 21 fantastic patterns that come with Photoshop. They are found in the Goodies/Patterns folders of the Photoshop application.

Let's modify an existing pattern and use it for a tiled background.

1. In the top menu bar, select File→Open and navigate your desktop to find the folder the Photoshop application is in.

2. Once you've found the folder, open the folders Goodies and then Patterns.

**3.** Open the India pattern (see Figure 8–10).

**FIGURE 8–10** The India pattern

**4.** Save the file and give it a new name, such as New_pattern.psd.

**5.** In the Layers palette create a new layer.

**6.** Drag the new layer below the bottom layer with the pattern.

**7.** While the new bottom blank layer is selected, choose a light color in your Web Safe palette, such as a yellow.

**8.** Fill the blank layer with the color you've chosen.

**9.** At the top of the Layers palette there is a layer control pull-down menu named "Normal."

**10.** Click on it and pull it down to Multiply (see Figure 8–11).

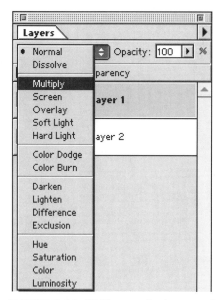

**FIGURE 8–11** Clicking on the Layers palette and selecting Multiply

11. You will now see the India pattern with a color behind it.

12. To lessen the contrast between the black and yellow, go to the Opacity selector in the Layers palette.

13. Either type in 15% or hold your cursor over the number and use the slider to select 15% (see Figure 8–12).

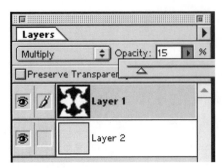

**FIGURE 8–12** Selecting the opacity for Layer 1

14. Now you have a pattern that is yellow and gold.

15. Follow the same HTML steps given earlier to place your new background image on a page.

16. Test it in a browser (see Figure 8–13).

## Creating New Patterns

Now that you have the basics of how a tile works, let's make one of our own. You can create an easy pattern that has a border, or one that is more free-formed.

BORDERED PATTERN

1. In the top menu bar, select File→New.

2. Create a page that is 72 pixels × 72 pixels.

3. Fill the background with a light color.

4. Draw a darker image in the center of the square (see Figure 8–14).

5. Now place a border around the image (see Figure 8–15).

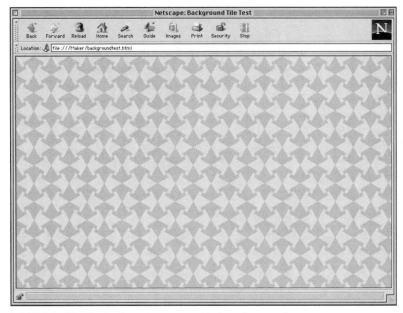

**FIGURE 8–13** The India pattern as a tiled background

**FIGURE 8–14** Draw a darker image in the center of the square

**FIGURE 8–15** Place a border around the image

6. Export the image as a GIF.

7. Use the image as a background the same way you did earlier.

8. Test your bordered pattern in a browser (see Figure 8–16).

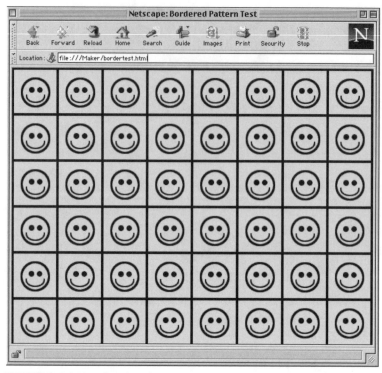

**FIGURE 8–16** Your bordered pattern as it appears in a browser

### FREE-FORMED PATTERN

The free-formed pattern takes a little more effort to create. To make it simple, we'll use filters to create the pattern. You can use the same effects shown next by drawing freehand shapes or using existing art.

1. In the top menu bar, select File→New.

2. Create a page that is 144 pixels × 144 pixels.

3. Fill the background with a dark color.

4. Think of the existing Photoshop patterns. Look again at Figure 8–9 to see how the patterns are set.

5. In the top menu bar, select Filter→Texture→Mosaic Tiles. The Mosaic Tiles dialog box will appear (see Figure 8–17).

6. In the top menu bar, select Filter→Other→Offset. Set the offset at Wrap Around and 80 and 80 (see Figure 8–18). Figure 8–19 shows the image after offset.

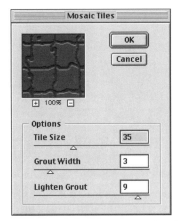

**FIGURE 8–17** The Mosaic Tiles dialog box

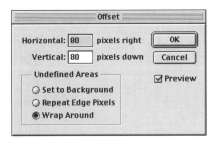

**FIGURE 8–18** Setting the offset at Wrap Around and 80 and 80

**FIGURE 8–19** Wrap Around at a setting of 80 and 80

**7.** You can test your image's tiling capabilities by selecting File→Select All in the top menu bar.

**8.** In the top menu bar, select Edit→Define Pattern (see Figure 8–20).

**9.** Create a new document at a larger size, such as 400 pixels × 400 pixels.

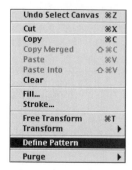

**FIGURE 8–20** Selecting Define Pattern from the top menu bar

**10.** In the top menu bar, select Edit→Fill and select Pattern (see Figure 8–21).

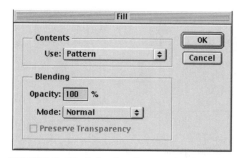

**FIGURE 8–21** Selecting Pattern in the Fill dialog box

**11.** Check and see if the tiling is done well. If not, go back and make adjustments with the Offset filter.

**12.** If the tiling works well, export the tile as a GIF.

**13.** Using the HTML code, use the new pattern as a background.

**14.** Test the new page in a browser.

## ◆ Checking Your Work

One of the biggest complaints about designing for the Web is that, unlike a printed brochure, no two people see your design in the same way. Each platform, browser, monitor, screen resolution, screen size, and bit depth will treat your site differently. There is also the speed of the modem connection to consider. With all these differences, there is one thing that stays the same: You have to test your site on all of these variables to make sure it will work for everyone. It's important to have access to as many platforms as possible running as many different browsers. Here are some possible explanations:

## Platform

There are inherent differences in the four most popular computer platforms. The Mac, PC, SUN, and SGI computers all display color differently. They each comprise different hardware and software. That doesn't even take into consideration that each monitor on the market is set to display color differently. If you aren't sure what we're talking about, go to a computer store that sells more than one type of computer. Often times they are all lined up next to each other with their monitors on. Look at the differences between all the computers and different monitors. Sometimes you can see major differences between two different setups with the same computer and monitor.

## Color Calibration and Contrast

It's not important to know the exact details of which platform does what to the color—there is just too much information to know, and that doesn't fit into the *essentials* category. What you need to know as a designer is that Macs display images lighter than PCs. Most designers are creating in a Mac environment and most users are seeing your work on a PC. That's a crucial piece of information to remember.

This is especially important for photographs. We've shown you how to become the office hero by cleaning up the CEO's face, but the last thing you want to hear from the CEO's office is, "Hey, you can't see my face because it's so dark. Who did this?"

If you create on the Mac, find a PC to test your design for image contrast, and vice versa.

## Type

Type is displayed in different fonts and at different sizes on both Macs and PCs for two reasons: The first is that the machine itself displays images on the monitor at different resolutions. The Mac displays images at 72 dots per inch (dpi). The PC resolution for the monitor is 96 dpi. That alone makes everything on the screen a little larger. You can test this by taking a screen capture on both platforms. Then open them up in Photoshop and check the image size. You will see these numbers in the resolution below the file size.

The second reason type displays differently on both platforms is that they each use a different default font. The Mac uses Times and the PC uses New Times Roman. They are similar, but New Times Roman has a larger "x" height, or is a little fatter top to bottom.

*Leading* (pronounced "ledding") is the distance between lines of type and is also different on the two platforms. The PC's leading appears wider than the Mac's.

The column widths are also displayed differently on Macs and PCs. Macs display more type across a column due to the font size and dpi issues.

So, trying to design so HTML type fits perfectly next to an image will not work on each browser. It might look good on your machine, but it won't be the same on others.

## Browsers

There are differences between browsers and the way they display the page. There are too many to cover, but some of the differences involve the top and left buffer spaces and image loading. The top and left buffer spaces before the page begins are different enough that if you are trying to align a background and a foreground image, they will not line up perfectly everywhere. You can get around that by using a line of code in place of your <BODY> tag. This removes the top and left margins so the page starts in the same spot on all browsers that support this feature.

```
<BODY MARGINWIDTH="0" MARGINHEIGHT="0"
LEFTMARGIN="0" TOPMARGIN="0">
```

## Browser Versions

Browser versions within the same browser, such as Netscape 3.0, 4.0, and 4.5, all display pages differently and have different features. Again, there are too many to discuss in an *Essential* guide. Test your pages on as many versions of each browser as you can on each platform.

## Screen Size

As you know, there are monitors from the size of a laptop all the way up to a 21" monitor. There are people surfing the Web on a

51" presentation monitor also. The pages you create have to look good on all size screens and all screen resolutions.

## Screen Resolution and Color Depth

Screen resolution is referred to in numbers, such as $640 \times 480$, $800 \times 600$, and $1024 \times 768$. These numbers are all in pixels. If the screen is at $640 \times 480$, that means the width of the screen is 640 pixels and the height is 480 pixels. Everything on the page appears larger than the other resolutions. Conversely, at 1024 pixels $\times$ 768 pixels, almost twice as much information is being displayed on the page because the screen is 1024 pixels wide. Everything on the page appears to be smaller and show more of the page.

When you are using type, remember that it will be seen at a greater size difference than what you may have planned for. If you are using 8-point type and it looks perfect on a $640 \times 480$ resolution, it may be a miniature blur at $1024 \times 768$. This is yet another reason to test your work at different screen resolutions.

Color depth refers to how many colors are being seen by the screen. Color depth is referred to in number of colors—256 colors, thousands or millions of colors. You could spend much more time learning about bit depth and what it means, but to get your job done, you need to know a couple of things about color depth.

In the same fashion that most designers use Macs and most surfers use PCs, most designers create images using a color depth of thousands or millions, while most surfers will see the images on 256-color machines.

This simply means that more colors are visible to you, the designer. An image can look significantly different in 256 colors. You see this mostly in places that have gradients or drop shadows. At 256 colors, you will see bands of color and not a smooth blend if done incorrectly. Also non-Web Safe colors look quite different on 256 and thousands of colors.

To change the screen resolution and color depth on a Mac, go to the Control Panel→Monitors and you will see Color Depth on the left and Resolution on the right. Experiment with different settings and check your pages.

To change your screen resolution and color depth on a Windows PC, go to the Properties display and click on the Settings tab. From there, you can change the Color Palette and Desktop Area. Again, experiment with different settings and check your pages.

One important note: Quit your browser before you change your color depth. For some reason, the color depth won't show true unless you quit your browser before making changes.

## RECAP

In this chapter, you learned some tips for creating temporary images to preload before main images. You learned how to create small images that clicked to a larger version of that same image. You also learned to use the HTML code to change the size of an image if necessary, or to create an interesting look. "Patterns" became more than just a word to you. Now you can create any pattern you want, whether it's a vertical navigation bar, a repeating bordered background pattern, or a repeating nonbordered background pattern. You also know how to test, test, test your work. We can't stress this part enough: You can never test too much.

## ADVANCED PROJECTS

1. Find a picture of a pretty outdoor scene. Create a separate low source black-and-white version and put both images on the page together. Watch how the page loads with the low to high source images.

2. Create a page with six 80-pixel × 80-pixel thumbnail images that load a low source image first.

3. Now, create pages for each thumbnail that show the larger image when the smaller image is clicked.

4. Create one image and display it on an HTML page at many sizes.

5. Create one image at 72 pixels × 72 pixels and display it at 400 pixels × 400 pixels on an HTML page.

6. Create a background vertical navigation bar with a width of 350 pixels.

7. Create a background that visually repeats across the whole image.

8. Create several different types of backgrounds.

9. Go create your own homepage with everything you know, using this book as a reference.

10. Check your work on a Mac and PC at all the suggested settings in this chapter.

# ◆ Go Forth and Prosper

You now have all the knowledge we can pass on to you—the rest is up to you. Do all the homework assignments and create new ones for yourself. As you know, the best way to learn is on deadline, when you are forced to learn at an amazing pace. This book was designed so that you can go back and use the sections as a reference. We've provided reference materials in the appendices as well. Remember to check out the companion Web site for the book at: http://www.phptr.com/essential. We'd love to hear how this book worked for you. Please send us feedback through the Web site.

Have fun creating!

# A Photoshop 5.0 Tools Reference

*Photoshop 5 has many tools with lots of options for each. Here's a list of them and what they do, in the order in which they appear on the tool bar.*

## Marquee Tools

All Marquee tools make regularly shaped selections. Hold down the Option/Alt key to draw your selection from the center, and hold down the Shift key to constrain the selection shape to a square or a circle. Hold down the Shift key and press M to toggle between the Rectangular and Elliptical Marquee tools.

### RECTANGULAR MARQUEE

**FIGURE A–1**

Creates a rectangular selection area.

### ELLIPTICAL MARQUEE

**FIGURE A–2**

Creates an elliptical selection area.

## SINGLE ROW AND SINGLE COLUMN MARQUEES

**FIGURE A–3**

These marquees create a 1-pixel wide selection area.

### MARQUEE OPTIONS

**Feathering:** Feathering lets you blur the edges of a selection by creating a border around the selected area that gradually fades into the surrounding pixels. The width of the feathered edge can range from 0 (for no feathering) to 250 pixels.

**Anti-aliased:** This only works with the Elliptical Marquee tool. Checking this box causes your selection to be anti-aliased. Anti-aliasing removes jagged edges by creating a subtle transition between the edges of the selection and the surrounding pixels.

**Style:** You have a choice of three styles:

1. Normal: No-constraints Marquee tool.
2. Constrained Aspect Ratio: Keeps the proportions of your selection constant, no matter what size your selection is.
3. Fixed size: Creates an exact-sized selection area based on the number of pixels you enter.

## *Crop*

**FIGURE A–4**

This tool allows you to trim an image; not just a layer, mind you, but the whole image.

### CROP OPTIONS

**Target Size:** You can trim and resize what you trimmed in a single step by checking the Fixed Target Size box. You can determine the height and width of the image once you've cropped it.

**Hinge:** New in version 5, small crosshairs appear in the middle of your crop selection. You can move these crosshairs around the image, and then rotate your crop selection around the crosshairs. Honestly, we haven't used this feature much.

## Move

**FIGURE A–5**

This tool simply moves the images on the selected area. Place your cursor inside a selected area and choose the Move tool. Now you can move the selected area around.

### MOVE OPTIONS

**Pixel Doubling:** Doubles the size of the layer's pixels for faster moving.

**Auto Select Layer:** Selecting this option lets Photoshop decide which layer you're trying to move. When you click on the image, Photoshop will select and move the upper-most visible layer at that point.

## Lasso Tools

### REGULAR

**FIGURE A–6**

The Regular Lasso lets you create a selection area by drawing a freehand shape.

### POLYGONAL

**FIGURE A–7**

The Polygonal Lasso lets you make a selection area with a series of straight-line segments. Holding down Option/Alt will let you draw in freehand mode.

## MAGNETIC

**FIGURE A–8**

The Magnetic Lasso is great. Use it to select a preexisting shape by simply clicking near the points on the shape you want, and Photoshop is smart enough to draw a selection area that follows the shape you're after.

### LASSO OPTIONS

**Feathering:** Feathering allows you to blur the edges of a selection by creating a border around the selected area that gradually fades into the surrounding pixels. The width of the feathered edge can range from 0 (for no feathering) to 250 pixels.

**Anti-aliased:** Checking this causes your selection to be anti-aliased.

## Magic Wand

**FIGURE A–9**

The magic wand lets you select areas based on adjacent color similarities.

### MAGIC WAND OPTIONS

**Tolerance:** Sets how similar colors must be to be included in the selection area. Enter a high tolerance to allow a broader range of colors to be selected, and a low tolerance for only very similar colors to be selected.

## Airbrush

**FIGURE A–10**

Paints soft-edged freehand lines.

## AIRBRUSH OPTIONS

**Blending Menu:** Includes "behind," not found in the Layer palette's Blending menu.

**Pressure:** Sets how fast the "paint" is applied to the image.

**Fade to:** Enter a number to determine how many pixels are traveled before that colors fades to either transparency or the background color.

## *Paintbrush*

**FIGURE A–11**

This tool paints a soft-edged freehand line (not as soft as the airbrush).

## PAINTBRUSH OPTIONS

**Blending Menu:** Includes "behind," not found in the Layer palette's Blending menu.

**Opacity:** Determines the transparency of the brush strokes.

**Fade:** Enter a number to determine how many pixels are traveled before that colors fades to either transparency or the background color.

**Wet Edges:** Simulates simple watercolor effects.

**Stylus:** If you have a pressure-sensitive stylus, you can determine whether increased pressure determines brush size, paint opacity, or color.

## *Stamp Tools*

These tools let you sample part of an image and paint that image on another layer or on an entirely different image. To use these stamps, Option/Alt-click on the image or layer from which you want to start copying. Then go to the layer or image you want to copy to and start painting. Crosshairs will appear to show you where the stamp is sampling from.

## STAMP OPTIONS

**Blending Menu:** Includes "behind," not found in the Layer palette's Blending menu.

**Opacity:** Determines the transparency of the applied paint.

**Use All Layers:** When you sample an image using the stamps, by default you are sampling only the pixels on the selected layer. If you select Use All Layers, the stamp will sample from all visible layers, not just the selected one.

**Aligned:** After you Option/Alt-click on an image with the stamp and start painting, you can lift your mouse and start painting again on the target layer or image. When you start painting again, you can have the crosshairs follow your moves or go back to their original position.

**Stylus:** If you have a pressure-sensitive stylus, you can determine whether increased pressure determines brush size or paint opacity.

### RUBBER STAMP

FIGURE A–12

This powerful tool lets you copy parts of one layer to other parts of that same layer or to other layers. You can even apply part of one image to another image using this tool. To use the Rubber Stamp, select the stamp and Option/Alt-click on the area you want to copy from. Then move the stamp to the layer or image you want to copy to and start painting.

### PATTERN STAMP

FIGURE A–13

This stamp lets you define your own pattern and then paint that pattern in the same image or in another image. To use the Pattern Stamp, first select the Rectangular Marquee tool and select a rectangular area of your image. Then go to Edit→Define Pattern. Select the Pattern Stamp and draw the pattern on the same image or on another image.

## History Brush

FIGURE A–14

This brush lets you revert part of your image to its most recently saved version. Paint over the part of your image you wish to revert.

### HISTORY BRUSH OPTIONS

**Blending Menu:** Includes "behind," not found in the Layer palette's Blending menu.

**Opacity:** Determines the transparency of the applied paint.

**Impressionist:** With this option selected, the History Brush drags and smears the pixels of the original image as you paint.

**Stylus:** If you have a pressure-sensitive stylus, you can determine whether increased pressure determines brush size or paint opacity.

**NOTE**

If you wish to free some memory for Photoshop you can choose to clear the stored data in the Clipboard, Patterns, or History. Go to Edit→Purge to clear the memory. This is a permanent deletion, so use it carefully. We never actually use this option because as soon as you clear something from memory, chances are you'll need it badly 10 minutes later.

## *Eraser*

FIGURE A–15

The Eraser deletes pixels from your image. If you have Preserve Transparency turned on for the selected layer, the parts of the layer you erase will be changed to the current background color.

### ERASER OPTIONS

**Eraser Type:** Paintbrush, Pencil, Airbrush, or Block. To cycle through these options, hold down the Shift key and press E.

**Opacity:** Determines the transparency of the erasing.

**Fade:** Enter a number to determine how many pixels are traveled before the eraser gradually fades out.

**Wet Edges:** Simulates simple watercolor effects.

**Erase to History:** Causes the Eraser to act exactly like the History Brush; it reverts part of your image to its previously saved version.

**Stylus:** If you have a pressure-sensitive stylus, you can determine whether increased pressure determines brush size or paint opacity.

## Pencil

FIGURE A–16

The Pencil lets you draw hard-edged, freehand lines.

### PENCIL OPTIONS

**Pencil Type:** Paintbrush, Pencil, Airbrush, or Block. To cycle through these options, hold down the Shift key and press E.

**Opacity:** Determines the transparency of the erasing.

**Fade:** Enter a number to determine how many pixels are traveled before the pencil gradually fades out to transparency or the background color.

**Auto Erase:** If you begin dragging over an area that contains the foreground color, the pencil will change it to the background color; otherwise, it will draw the foreground color.

**Stylus:** If you have a pressure-sensitive stylus, you can determine whether increased pressure determines brush size or paint opacity.

## Line Tool

FIGURE A–17

The Line tool draws straight lines. Pretty simple.

## LINE TOOL OPTIONS

**Blending Menu:** Includes "behind," not found in the Layer palette's Blending menu.

**Opacity:** Determines the transparency of the paint.

**Weight:** The width of the line.

**Anti-aliased:** Whether the line is anti-aliased or not.

**Arrowheads:** You can specify whether the line has arrowheads at the beginning or end of the line (or both). If you decide you want an arrowhead, you can then determine the shape of the arrowhead by pressing the Shape button. Arrowhead sizes are determined as a percentage of the line width (the Weight option you entered earlier).

## *Focus Tools: Blur, Sharpen, Smudge*

These tools alter the focus, or clarity, of parts of an image.

## FOCUS TOOL OPTIONS

**Blending Menu:** Includes "behind," not found in the Layer palette's Blending menu.

**Opacity:** Determines the transparency of the applied paint.

**Use All Layers:** When you sample an image using the Focus tools, by default you are sampling only the pixels on the selected layer. If you select Use All Layers, the tool will sample from all visible layers, not just the selected one.

**Finger Painting:** This option is only available with the Smudge tool. It drops a dab of the foreground color into the image as you begin to smudge.

**Stylus:** If you have a pressure-sensitive stylus, you can determine whether increased pressure determines brush size or pressure of the tool on the image.

## BLUR

**FIGURE A–18**

The Blur tool softens edges and reduces detail in an image. You can also blur an image using one of the Blur filters.

## SHARPEN

**FIGURE A–19**

The Sharpen tool brings soft edges into focus. You can also sharpen an image by using one of the Sharpen filters.

## SMUDGE

**FIGURE A–20**

The Smudge tool acts as if the pixels are wet paint and you're dragging your finger through it. This one is especially fun with a stylus.

## *Toning Tools: Dodge, Burn, Sponge*

The Toning tools allow you to lighten, darken, and change the color saturation of your image. The names "dodge" and "burn" and the shapes of the icons come from the methods used by photographers to lighten and darken certain areas of a photograph by changing exposure time.

### TONING TOOL OPTIONS

**Tone to Affect:** For the Dodge and Burn tools, select the range of pixels that you want to affect: "shadows" for darker pixels, "midtones" for the middle range of grays, or "highlights" for lighter pixels.

**De/Saturation:** For the Sponge tool, this option determines whether the sponge is adding or taking away color saturation.

**Exposure/Pressure:** Determines how strongly the tool acts on the image. Dodge and Burn use Exposure, while Sponge uses Pressure.

**Stylus:** If you have a pressure-sensitive stylus, you can determine whether increased pressure determines brush size or exposure/pressure of the tool on the image.

### DODGE

**FIGURE A–21**

The Dodge tool lightens an image.

### BURN

**FIGURE A–22**

The Burn tool darkens an image.

### SPONGE

**FIGURE A–23**

The Sponge tool increases or decreases an image's color saturation. If it's a grayscale image, the Sponge tool can increase or decrease the contrast by moving gray levels closer or further from the middle gray.

## Pen Tools

Although still a far cry from Adobe Illustrator's pens, Photoshop's pen tools are quite helpful, and are perfectly adequate for simple jobs. Using the Pen tools is more complex than simply using the Paintbrush or the Pencil, but the learning curve is worth it.

### REGULAR PEN

**FIGURE A–24**

The Regular Pen tool allows you to create straight lines and smooth, flowing curves. These pen lines can then be converted into drawn lines, selection areas, or filled areas.

## REGULAR PEN OPTIONS

**Rubber Band:** Lets you preview the proposed path as you draw. Otherwise, you only see the path segment when you choose a point by pressing the mouse button.

## MAGNETIC PEN

FIGURE A–25

The Magnetic Pen allows you to draw around an image. Photoshop then looks for what you're mostly likely trying to draw around and places the images and direction points to match the image.

## FREEFORM PEN

FIGURE A–26

Use the Freeform Pen to create a curve by simply drawing the curve you want. After you draw your curve, it's transformed into a path, which is usually smoother than the curve you drew (unless you have steadier hands than we do).

## ADD ANCHOR POINT

FIGURE A–27

The Add Anchor Point tool lets you add an anchor point to a pre-existing path.

## DELETE ANCHOR POINT

FIGURE A–28

The Delete Anchor Point tool lets you delete an anchor point to a preexisting path.

## DIRECT SELECTION

**FIGURE A–29**

The Direct Selection tool allows you to move individual anchor points or direction points on a path.

### CONVERT ANCHOR POINT

**FIGURE A–30**

The Convert Anchor Point tool lets you convert an anchor point from a smooth point to a corner point, and vice versa.

## Type Tools: Type, Type Mask, Vertical Type, Vertical Type Mask

**FIGURE A–31**

The Type tools allow for much more ease of use and control in version 5 than version 4. Make sure you download patch 5.0.2 from the Adobe site (http://www.adobe.com)—among other things, it fixes some problems with kerning.

The Type and Vertical Type tools let you create colored type in a new layer. The Type Mask and Vertical Type Mask tools create selections in the shape of the type. These selections appear on the active layer.

All of the Type tools use a dialog box with several options.

### TYPE TOOL DIALOG BOX

Font: Choose the font you want. Unlike Photoshop 4, version 5 drops the possibility of stylizing your text. That is, fonts often come with several versions: bold, italic, condensed, and so on. If you don't have those font versions (which are separate fonts in themselves), Photoshop 4 lets you create your own bold or italic version of the fonts. Photoshop 5 doesn't, and that actually makes life easier for print designs, since stylized fonts often don't display the way they should. It doesn't matter to Web designers.

**Font:** To start typing in a font, select the font, click in the main box, and start typing. To change some characters to a specific font, highlight those characters and choose a different font. You can choose from available type styles in the menu to the right of the Fonts menu.

**Size:** You can choose the size of the font, as well as the measurement unit. As a Web designer, both measurement units (points and pixels) are interchangeable because you're working in a 72 dpi resolution; 40 pixels will result in the same size text as 40 points. If you start to work in a different resolution, like 300 dpi, whether you use pixels or points makes a huge difference.

**Kerning:** Controls the spacing between two characters. You can control kerning manually or set it to whatever the font designer built into the font by checking the Auto Kern box. For example, the font designer probably set the space between an A and a W to be less than the space between an A and an F.

**Color:** Clicking on the color opens up the Adobe Color Picker, allowing you to choose any color.

**Leading:** Specifies the spacing between baselines. This spacing is measured with the same units you specify in the Size section.

**Tracking:** Inserts uniform space in between more than two characters. Use tracking to adjust the spacing of a word or a block of text.

**Baseline:** Adjusts the baseline shift of the type. Baseline shift is the distance the type appears from the baseline. This lowers or raises the text to produce subscripts or superscripts. The baseline shift is measured in the units you specify next to the Size box.

**Alignment:** Aligns the text to the left, right, or center, according to where the insertion point (the I-beam cursor) is.

**Preview:** Displays the type in the image.

**Auto Kern:** Uses the kerning designated by the font designer. Unchecking this allows you to control kerning manually.

**Anti-aliased:** Lets you specify smooth-edged text.

**Rotate:** Used when creating vertical type, this option rotates the individual characters 90°.

**Zoom Buttons:** Allow you to magnify your type.

**Fit in Window:** Fits whatever you've typed into the visible window available. Checking this option turns off the Zoom buttons.

### OTHER TYPE GOODIES

Go to Layer→Type for more options:

**Render Layer:** Transforms your type in a regular layer. You won't be able to edit the text after you render the layer, but you will be able to use filters on the image, which is forbidden on a type layer.

**Horizontal:** Makes type horizontal.

**Vertical:** Makes type vertical.

If you venture into Layer→Effects, you can apply effects on your type, such as drop shadows and inner and outer bevels. When you change the text on a layer, any effects on that layer will automatically change to reflect the type changes. These effects are also available for most nontype layers, but are especially handy for type layers. These effects are covered at length in Appendix B, "Photoshop 5.0 Extras Reference."

## *Measure*

FIGURE A–32

When you drag the Measure tool from one point to another, a nonprinting temporary line is drawn, and the following information is shown in the Info palette:

**Starting Location:** (X and Y).

**Angle:** Degrees measured from a horizontal 0° line, and increasing in angle in a counterclockwise direction (A).

**Distance:** Direct distance between the two points (D).

**Width and Height:** The horizontal and vertical distance between the two points (W and H).

**Protractor:** You can use the Measure tool as a protractor by Option/Alt-clicking on one end of the measure line and drawing another measure line. The angle between the lines is calculated, as well as the distance of the two lines (D1 and D2).

## Gradient Tools: Linear, Radial, Angular, Reflected, Diamond

The Gradient tools create gradual blends between multiple colors. There are many preset color blends, or you can create your own with the Gradient Editor. The Gradient Editor is discussed in Appendix B.

### GRADIENT TOOL OPTIONS

**Blending Menu:** Includes "behind," not found in the Layer palette's Blending menu.

**Opacity:** Determines the transparency of the gradient.

**Gradient Type:** Allows you to select a preset gradient.

**Transparency:** If you've created a gradient with some transparency in it, you can turn that transparency on or off.

**Dither:** Creates a smoother blend with less banding.

**Reverse:** Reverses the order of the color blends.

### LINEAR

FIGURE A–33

The Linear gradient tool shades from the start point to the end point in a straight line. It's usually used with the foreground color fading into the background color.

### RADIAL

FIGURE A–34

The Radial gradient tool shades from the start point to the end point in a circular fashion. It's useful for creating quick, 3D-type shading for circular forms.

## ANGULAR

**FIGURE A-35**

The Angular gradient tool shades from the start point to the end point in a counterclockwise sweep.

## REFLECTED

**FIGURE A-36**

The Reflected gradient tool shades from the start point to the end point back to the start point.

## DIAMOND

**FIGURE A-37**

The Diamond gradient tool shades from the start point to the end point in a diamond pattern. The start point is in the middle of the diamond, with the end point at the corners.

## *Paint Bucket*

**FIGURE A-38**

The Paint Bucket tool fills adjacent pixels with the foreground color or a pattern, if you've defined one.

### PAINT BUCKET OPTIONS

**Blending Menu:** Includes "behind," not found in the Layer palette's Blending menu.

**Opacity:** Determines the transparency of the gradient.

**Tolerance:** Sets how similar colors must be to be included in the selection area. Enter in a high tolerance to allow a broader range of colors to be selected, and a low tolerance for only very similar colors to be selected.

**Anti-aliased:** Lets you specify smooth-edged borders to the paint fill.

**Contents:** Paints adjacent pixels with either the foreground color or a pattern, if you've defined one.

**Use All Layers:** Fills pixels based on the merged color data from all visible layers.

## Color Preview Tools: Eyedropper, Color Sampler

**FIGURE A–39**

The Eyedropper tool lets you see the color value of up to four different areas at once, and make one of those colors the foreground.

### COLOR PREVIEW TOOLS OPTIONS

**Sample Size:** Can be one of the three options: 1) point sample, which is a single pixel; 2) a 3-pixel × 3-pixel color average; 3) a 5-pixel × 5-pixel color average.

## Hand

**FIGURE A–40**

The Hand tool moves the entire image within the viewable area. It's useful when you're at a high magnification and want to see another part of the image.

## *Zoom*

**FIGURE A–41**

The Zoom tool magnifies your image to the next preset percentage. Holding down Option/Alt demagnifies (zooms out) your image to the next preset percentage. Double-clicking on the Zoom tool will bring your image to 100% magnification. You can also use the Zoom tool like the Marquee tool and select an area to magnify.

# B Photoshop 5.0 Extras Reference

*Photoshop 5.0 has some great new features, including Layer Effects and Adjustment Layers, along with the still-great holdover from version 4, the Gradient Editor. Here they are:*

## ◆ Layer Effects

Layer Effects are automated effects you can apply to any Photoshop layer. The effects are Drop Shadow, Inner Shadow, Inner and Outer Glows, Inner and Outer Beveling, Embossing, and Pillow Embossing. The neat thing about these effects, besides being automatic, is the fact that they're tied to the layer's contents, so if you make a change in the layer, the effect automatically adjusts. For example, if you have a circle with a drop shadow effect and you use the Eraser to remove part of the circle, the drop shadow will adjust to reflect the new circle shape. This also occurs when you apply a layer mask to the layer.

When you apply Layer Effects, a small black circle with an "f" in it appears next to the layer name in the Layers palette. You can access that layer's effects by double-clicking on the icon.

You can also apply Layer Effects to type layers, which is a huge time-saver.

You can achieve interesting results by applying an effect to a layer and then erasing parts of the layer with the Eraser set to 50% opacity.

To get to the effects, go to Layer→Effects and choose one. You can apply more than one effect to any layer.

### Drop Shadow

Drop Shadow creates a copy of your layer below the selected layer, and blurs it to create a shadow effect. Select the layer you want and choose Layer→Effects→Drop Shadow. You can place the shadow by entering values in the option boxes or by dragging the shadow (using arrows to move the shadow pixel by pixel won't work) in the image. The distance and angles are updated automatically.

### Inner Shadow

This effect works in the same way as the Drop Shadow, except that the shadow is placed above the image and only shows up inside the layer's boundaries. This effect makes the layer look like it's on a piece of paper below all the layers, which have been cut away to reveal the active layer.

### Inner/Outer Glows

These effects create glows on the inside or outside of your image. For inner glow, you have the option of the glow emanate from the center of the images or the edges. If you're not seeing the effect you expected, try cranking up the blur and increasing the effect intensity.

### Inner/Outer Bevel and Embossing

The Bevel and Emboss effects are rolled into the Bevel and Emboss option. You choose which effect you want from a pull-down menu near the bottom of the dialog box. Two elements are needed to determine any bevel or emboss: highlight and shadow. Both beveling and embossing mimic the effect of light shining on your image, necessitating highlight and shadow.

> **Depth:** Sets how accentuated the bevel or emboss is (this is similar to the Intensity setting in other effects).
> **Up/Down:** Sets the position of the highlight.

### Options Common to Most Effects

> **Apply:** Tells Photoshop if you want to apply this layer once you click the OK button.
> **Mode:** This option determines how the layer effects will interact with the underlying layer, but not necessarily the

layer the effect is a part of. An inner shadow effect will interact with the active layer because it's drawn on top of the layer, but a drop shadow won't because it's drawn below. Actually, Photoshop has default values for each effect's mode, and those are the ones we usually end up using.

**Opacity:** Sets the amount of transparency of the layer effect.

**Color:** Lets you choose the color by launching the Color Picker.

**Angle:** Sets the angle at which the effect is applied. You can choose either a *local* angle, which will be used for only that effect, or a *global* angle.

**Global Angle:** You can set an angle to which all of the effects will be applied. This is useful if you a have a number of layers with effects on them and want to play with different light sources. Go to Layer→Effects→Global Angle to set this value.

**Blur:** Diffuses the edges of the effect for a softer look.

**Intensity:** Sets the strength at which the effect is applied.

# ◆ Adjustment Layers

Adjustment layers are special layers that don't contain any pixels, but affect the tone and colors of all the layers below them. This allows you to experiment with different tone and color adjustments without changing any of the pixels in the other layers. You can also create an adjustment layer that affects only the layer below it or affects only a clipping group.

Adjustment layers act like regular layers in that they can be moved, deleted, hidden, and copied like any other layer. However, each adjustment layer can have only one type of adjustment: Levels, Curves, Brightness/Contrast, Color Balance, Hue/Saturation, Selective Color, Channel Mixer, Invert, Threshold, and Posterize. You can recognize an adjustment layer by a half-filled circle next to the layer name in the Layers palette.

## Creating an Adjustment Layer

Option/Alt-click on the New Layer icon in the Layers palette, or choose Layer→New→New Adjustment Layer.

### Editing an Adjustment Layer

Once you've created an adjustment layer, you can't change its adjustment mode. For example, if you've created a Levels adjustment layer, you can't change it to an Invert adjustment layer—you have to create a whole new adjustment layer.

However, you can alter the layer's settings by either double-clicking on the layer in the Layers palette, or by going to Layer→Adjustment Options.

### Editing an Adjustment Layer Mask

Adjustment layers are also layer masks. Therefore, by painting on them or erasing them you can select which parts of the underlying image are affected by the adjustment.

1. Shift-clicking on the adjustment layer's thumbnail will temporarily hide the layer's effects. Click on the thumbnail again to redisplay the adjustment (this also works on regular layer masks).
2. Option/Alt-clicking on the thumbnail will display only the grayscale mask in the image window. You can alter, paint, copy, and paste this grayscale image as you would another image. Option/Alt-click on the thumbnail to display the other layers.
3. Shift-Option/Alt-click will display the layer mask in rubylith mode (where the layer mask appears in pink over the image). Shift-Option/Alt-click again to display the other layers.

Combining a layer with effects and a layer mask with an adjustment layer with the same mask can create some really interesting results.

## ◆ The Gradient Editor

The Gradient Editor allows you to create your own color blends or modify existing gradients for use with any of the Gradient tools (see Appendix A, "Photoshop 5.0 Tools Reference"). To launch the Gradient Editor, bring up the Options palette for any of the Gradient tools and press the Edit button (see Figure B–1).

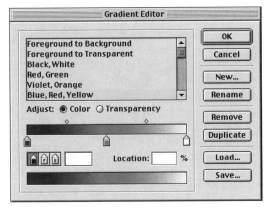

**FIGURE B–1** The Gradient Editor dialog box

To create a new gradient, click the New button. To create a new gradient based on an existing one, select the gradient you want and click Duplicate. To edit an existing gradient, just select it in the list. And then get ready.

## Changing Colors

- To choose the starting color, click on the left-most color stop (the item that looks like a little marker below the first gradient line). The triangular part of the color stop turns black, indicating that you're modifying that color stop.
- To change the color, double-click the color stop or click in the color swatch below the gradient bar. This calls the Color Picker.
- To make your chosen color stops to match the current foreground, click on the color stop you wish to change and then click the foreground selection box, which is in the box of three markers below the gradient and next to the color swatch. The marker with the F is the foreground selection box and the marker with the B is the background color selection box.
- You can also choose a color by positioning the cursor over the gradient itself. It turns into the Eyedropper and the color you click on appears in the color swatch.

## Adding and Deleting Colors

- To add colors to the gradient, click below the gradient. A new color stop will appear with the color that's in the color swatch.
- To delete a color stop, simply drag it away from the gradient—it will disappear.

## Adjusting Placement

- You can move color stops by simply dragging them along the gradient, even past other color stops.
- Adjust the midpoints of the gradient by dragging the little diamonds on the top of the gradient. A midpoint is the point between two colors in a gradient where the color mix is 50% of the starting color and 50% of the ending color.

## Transparency

You can also adjust a gradient's transparency separately from its color composition. Click Transparency next to Adjust and you'll be presented with a gradient different from the one you used to experiment with color.

Adding, modifying, and deleting different spots and values of transparency works much like adjusting the color blend. To determine a transparency spot, enter its opacity. The transparency spots and midpoints can be moved in the same way as the color stops and midpoints.

# C Photoshop 5.0 Filters Reference

*The artistic possibilities available with the myriad Photoshop 5 filters are infinite, so don't try to memorize them all. Experiment with the different filters. You may not always create exactly what you're looking for, but you may come up with something better. You may also find some great filters for future projects. Trust us on this one. Now get in there and start experimenting.*

For all of these filters, we're going to use the same base image (see Figure C–1). Our foreground color is orange and our background color is a moss green (see Figure C–2).

Obviously, you can't get the full effect of these filters in black and white, but you can use this reference as a starting point.

We've organized the filters in the same way Adobe has:

- Artistic
- Blur
- Brush Strokes
- Distort
- Noise
- Pixelate
- Render
- Sharpen
- Sketch
- Stylize
- Texture

---

Material taken from Help description of Photoshop plug-ins from Adobe Photoshop 5.0. Reprinted by permission of Adobe Systems Incorporated. Adobe and Photoshop are trademarks of Adobe Systems Incorporated.

**FIGURE C–1** Our original image

**FIGURE C–2** Foreground and background colors

- Video
- Other

The filter descriptions in the following sections are straight from the Adobe Help feature that accompanies the program. Don't let that put you off—they're great.

# ◆ Artistic Filters

Choose a filter from the Artistic submenu to achieve a painterly or special effect for a fine arts or commercial project. For example, use the Cutout filter for collages or type treatment. These filters replicate natural or traditional media effects.

## COLORED PENCIL

The Colored Pencil filter draws an image using colored pencils on a solid background. Important edges are retained and given a rough crosshatch appearance; the solid background color shows through the smoother areas.

For a parchment effect, change the background color before applying the filter to a selected area (see Figures C–3 and C–4).

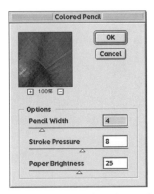

**FIGURE C–3** Colored Pencil dialog box

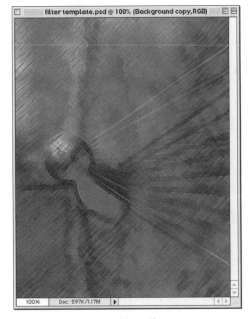

**FIGURE C–4** Colored Pencil

## CUTOUT

The Cutout filter portrays an image as though it were made from roughly cut-out pieces of colored paper. High-contrast images appear as if in silhouette, while colored images are built up from several layers of colored paper (see Figures C–5 and C–6).

**FIGURE C–5** Cutout dialog box

**FIGURE C–6** Cutout

## DRY BRUSH

This filter paints the edges of the image using a dry brush technique (between oil and watercolor). It simplifies an image by reducing its range of colors to areas of common color (see Figures C–7 and C–8).

**FIGURE C–7** Dry Brush dialog box

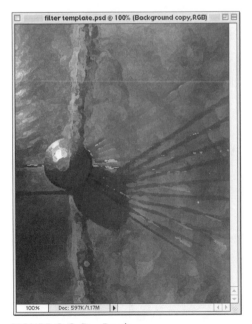

**FIGURE C–8** Dry Brush

## FILM GRAIN

The Film Grain filter applies an even pattern to the shadow tones and midtones of an image. A smoother, more saturated pattern is added to the image's lighter areas. This filter is useful for eliminating banding in blends and visually unifying elements from various sources (see Figures C–9 and C–10).

**FIGURE C–9** Film Grain dialog box

**FIGURE C–10** Film Grain

## FRESCO

The Fresco filter paints an image in a coarse style using short, rounded, and hastily applied dabs (see Figures C–11 and C–12).

**FIGURE C–11** Fresco dialog box

**FIGURE C–12** Fresco

## NEON GLOW

The Neon Glow filter adds various types of glows to the objects in an image and is useful for colorizing an image while softening its look. To select a glow color, click the Glow box and select a color from the color picker (see Figures C–13 and C–14).

**FIGURE C–13** Neon Glow dialog box

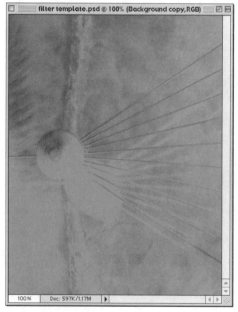

**FIGURE C–14** Neon Glow

## PAINT DAUBS

The Paint Daubs filter lets you choose from various brush sizes (from 1 to 50) and types for a painterly effect. Brush types include simple, light rough, light dark, wide sharp, wide blurry, and sparkle (see Figures C–15 and C–16).

**FIGURE C–15** Paint Daubs dialog box

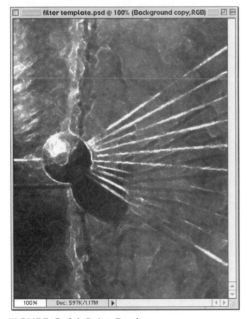

**FIGURE C–16** Paint Daubs

## PALETTE KNIFE

This filter reduces detail in an image to give the effect of a thinly painted canvas that reveals the texture underneath (see Figures C–17 and C–18).

**FIGURE C–17** Palette Knife dialog box

**FIGURE C–18** Palette Knife

## PLASTIC WRAP

The Plastic Wrap filter coats the image in shiny plastic, accentu-ating the surface detail (see Figures C–19 and C–20).

**FIGURE C–19** Plastic Wrap dialog box

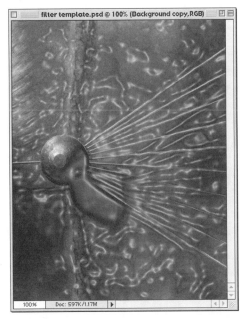

**FIGURE C–20** Plastic Wrap

## POSTER EDGES

The Poster Edges filter reduces the number of colors (posterizes) in an image according to the posterization option you set, finds the edges of the image, and draws black lines on them. Large, broad areas of the image have simple shading, while fine, dark detail is distributed throughout the image (see Figures C–21 and C–22).

**FIGURE C–21** Poster Edges dialog box

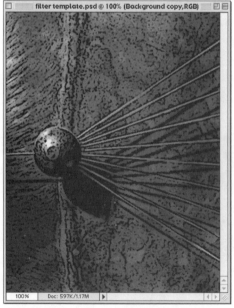

**FIGURE C–22** Poster Edges

## ROUGH PASTELS

This filter makes an image appear as if stroked with colored pastel chalk on a textured background. In areas of bright color, the chalk appears thick with little texture; in darker areas, the chalk appears scraped off to reveal the texture (see Figures C–23 and C–24).

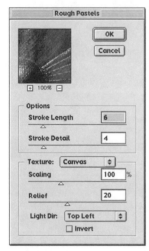

**FIGURE C–23**  Rough Pastels dialog box

**FIGURE C–24**  Rough Pastels

## SMUDGE STICK

The Smudge Stick filter softens an image using short diagonal strokes to smudge or smear the darker areas. Lighter areas become brighter and lose detail (see Figures C–25 and C–26).

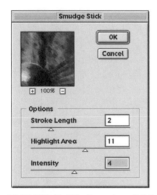

**FIGURE C–25** Smudge Stick dialog box

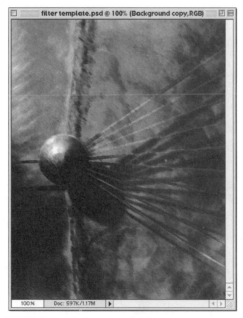

**FIGURE C–26** Smudge Stick

## SPONGE

The Sponge filter creates images with highly textured areas of contrasting color, which appear as if they were painted with a sponge (see Figures C–27 and C–28).

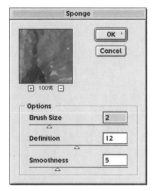

**FIGURE C–27** Sponge dialog box

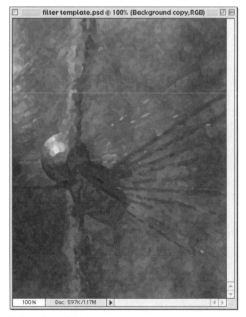

**FIGURE C–28** Sponge

## UNDERPAINTING

This filter paints the image on a textured background, and then paints the final image over it (see Figures C–29 and C–30).

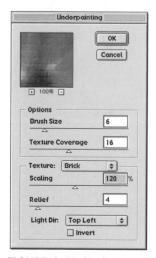

**FIGURE C–29** Underpainting dialog box

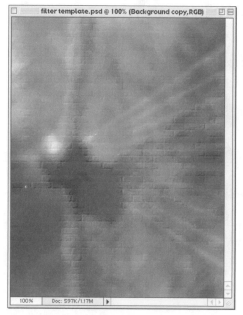

**FIGURE C–30** Underpainting

## WATERCOLOR

The Watercolor filter paints the image in a watercolor style, simplifying details in an image, using a medium brush loaded with water and color. Where significant tonal changes occur at edges, the filter saturates the color (see Figures C–31 and C–32).

**FIGURE C–31** Watercolor dialog box

**FIGURE C–32** Watercolor

# ◆ Blur

The six blur filters soften a selection or an image, and are useful for retouching. They smooth transitions by averaging the pixels next to the hard edges of defined lines and shaded areas in an image.

### BLUR AND BLUR MORE

The Blur and Blur More filters eliminate noise where significant color transitions occur in an image. The Blur filter smooths transitions by averaging the pixels next to the hard edges of defined lines and shaded areas. The Blur More filter produces an effect three or four times stronger than that of the Blur filter (see Figures C–33 and C–34).

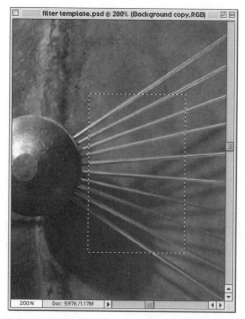

**FIGURE C–33** Blur

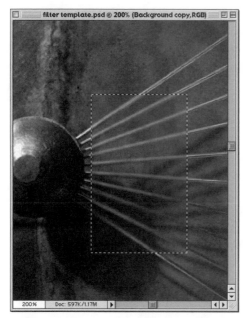

**FIGURE C-34** Blur More

## GAUSSIAN BLUR

The Gaussian Blur filter quickly blurs a selection by an adjustable amount. *Gaussian* refers to the bell-shaped curve that is generated when Adobe Photoshop applies a weighted average to the pixels. This filter adds low-frequency detail and can produce a hazy effect (see Figures C–35 and C–36).

**FIGURE C–35** Gaussian Blur dialog box

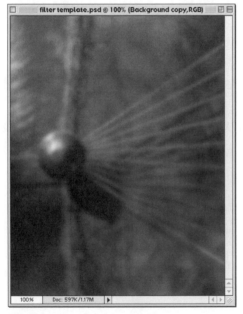

**FIGURE C–36** Gaussian Blur

## MOTION BLUR

This filter blurs in a particular direction (from –360° to +360°) and at a specific intensity (from 1 to 999). The effect is analogous to taking a picture of a moving object with a fixed exposure time (see Figures C–37 and C–38).

**FIGURE C–37** Motion Blur dialog box

**FIGURE C–38** Motion Blur

## RADIAL BLUR

The Radial Blur filter simulates the blur of a zooming or rotating camera to produce a soft blur. Choose Spin to blur along concentric circular lines, and then specify a degree of rotation; or choose Zoom to blur along radial lines, as if zooming in or out of the image, and specify an amount from 1 to 100. Blur quality ranges from Draft for the fastest but grainy results; or Good and Best for smoother results, which are indistinguishable except on a large selection. Specify the origin of the blur by dragging the pattern in the Blur Center box (see Figures C–39 and C–40).

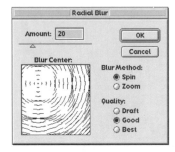

**FIGURE C–39** Radial Blur dialog box

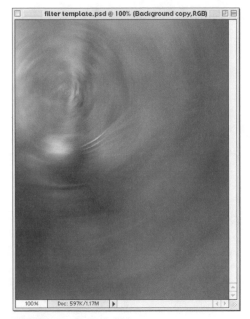

**FIGURE C–40** Radial Blur

## SMART BLUR

The Smart Blur filter precisely blurs an image. You can specify a radius to determine how far the filter searches for dissimilar pixels to blur; you can specify a threshold to determine how different the pixels' values should be before they are eliminated; and you can specify a blur quality. You also can set a mode for the entire selection (Normal), or for the edges of color transitions (Edge Only and Overlay). Where significant contrast occurs, Edge Only applies black-and-white edges and Overlay applies white (see Figures C–41 and C–42).

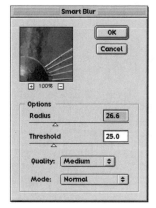

**FIGURE C–41** Smart Blur dialog box

**FIGURE C–42** Smart Blur

# ◆ Brush Stroke Filters

Like the Artistic filters, the Brush Stroke filters give a painterly or fine-arts look using different brush and ink stroke effects. Some of the filters add grain, paint, noise, edge detail, or texture to an image for a pointillist effect.

## ACCENTED EDGES

This filter accentuates the edges of an image. When the Edge Brightness control is set to a high value, the accents resemble white chalk; when set to a low value, the accents resemble black ink (see Figures C–43 and C–44).

**FIGURE C–43** Accented Edges dialog box

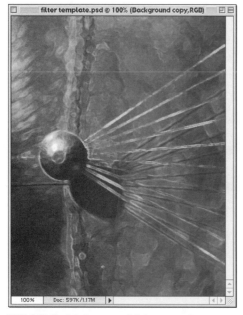

**FIGURE C–44** Accented Edges

## ANGLED STROKES

The Angled Strokes filter repaints an image using diagonal strokes. The lighter areas of the image are painted in strokes going in one direction, while the darker areas are painted in strokes going in the opposite direction (see Figures C–45 and C–46).

**FIGURE C–45** Angled Strokes dialog box

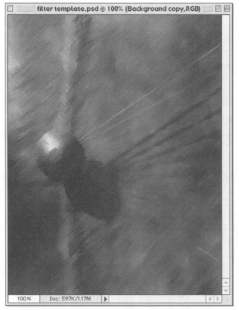

**FIGURE C–46** Angled Strokes

## CROSSHATCH

The Crosshatch filter preserves the details and features of the original image while adding texture and roughening the edges of the colored areas in the image with simulated pencil hatching. The Strength option controls the number of hatching passes, from 1 to 3 (see Figures C–47 and C–48).

**FIGURE C–47** Crosshatch dialog box

**FIGURE C–48** Crosshatch

## DARK STROKES

This filter paints dark areas of an image closer to black with short, tight strokes, and paints lighter areas of the image with long, white strokes (see Figures C–49 and C–50).

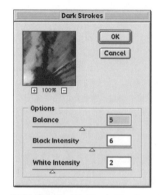

**FIGURE C–49** Dark Strokes dialog box

**FIGURE C–50** Dark Strokes

## INK OUTLINES

The Ink Outlines filter redraws an image with fine, narrow lines over the original details, in pen-and-ink style (see Figures C–51 and C–52).

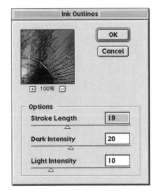

**FIGURE C–51** Ink Outlines dialog box

**FIGURE C–52** Ink Outlines

## SPATTER

The Spatter filter replicates the effect of a spatter airbrush. Increasing the options simplifies the overall effect (see Figures C–53 and C–54).

**FIGURE C–53** Spatter dialog box

**FIGURE C–54** Spatter

## SPRAYED STROKES

This filter repaints an image using its dominant colors with angled, sprayed strokes of color (see Figures C–55 and C–56).

**FIGURE C–55** Sprayed Strokes dialog box

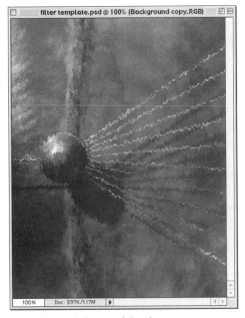

**FIGURE C–56** Sprayed Strokes

## SUMI-E

The Sumi-e filter paints an image in Japanese style as if with a wet brush full of black ink on rice paper. The effect is soft, blurry edges with rich blacks (see Figures C–57 and C–58).

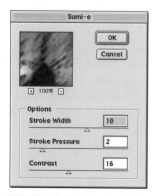

**FIGURE C–57** Sumi-e dialog box

**FIGURE C–58** Sumi-e

# ◆ Distort Filters

The Distort filters geometrically distort an image, creating 3-D or other reshaping effects. Note that these filters can be very memory intensive.

### DIFFUSE GLOW

The Diffuse Glow filter renders an image as though it were viewed through a soft diffusion filter. The filter adds see-through white noise to an image, with the glow fading from the center of a selection (see Figures C–59 and C–60).

**FIGURE C–59** Diffuse Glow dialog box

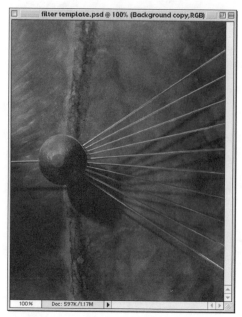

**FIGURE C–60** Diffuse Glow

## DISPLACE

Displace uses an image, called a *displacement map*, to determine how to distort a selection. For example, using a parabola-shaped displacement map, you can create an image that appears to be printed on a cloth held at its corners (see Figures C–61 and C–62).

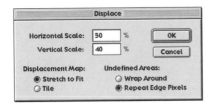

**FIGURE C–61** Displace dialog box

**FIGURE C–62** Displace

Create displacements maps using a flattened file saved in Adobe Photoshop format (except Bitmap mode images) or one that is saved with the Include Composite Image With Layered Files option turned on in the Saving Files preferences. You can also use the files included with your software (search for the Dispmaps folder in Windows or the Displacement Maps folder in Mac OS).

USING THE DISPLACE FILTER:

1. Choose Filter→Distort→Displace.
2. Enter the scale for the magnitude of the displacement. When the horizontal and vertical scales are set to 100%, the greatest displacement is 128 pixels (because middle gray produces no displacement).
3. If the displacement map is not the same size as the selection, choose how the map will fit the image. Stretch to Fit to resize the map, or Tile to fill the selection by repeating the map in a pattern.
4. Choose Wrap Around or Repeat Edge Pixels to determine how undistorted areas of the image will be treated.
5. Click OK.
6. Select and open the displacement map. The distortion is applied to the image.

The Displace filter shifts a selection using a color value from the displacement map: 0 is the maximum negative shift, 255 is the maximum positive shift, and a gray value of 128 produces no displacement. If a map has one channel, the image shifts along a diagonal defined by the horizontal and vertical scale ratios. If the map has more than one channel, the first channel controls the horizontal displacement, and the second channel controls the vertical displacement.

## GLASS

This filter makes an image appear as if it is being viewed through different types of glass. You can choose a glass effect or create your own glass surface as a Photoshop file, and apply it. You can adjust scaling, distortion, and smoothness settings. When using surface controls with a file, follow the instructions for the Displace filter (see Figures C–63 and C–64).

**FIGURE C–63** Glass dialog box

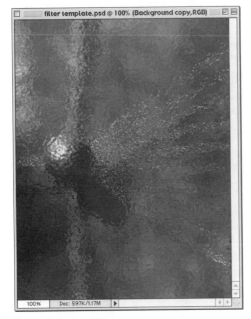

**FIGURE C–64** Glass

## OCEAN RIPPLE

The Ocean Ripple filter adds randomly spaced ripples to the image's surface, making the image look as if it were under water (see Figures C–65 and C–66).

**FIGURE C–65** Ocean Ripple dialog box

**FIGURE C–66** Ocean Ripple

## PINCH

The Pinch filter squeezes a selection. A positive value up to 100% shifts a selection inward; a negative value up to –100% shifts a selection outward (see Figures C–67 and C–68).

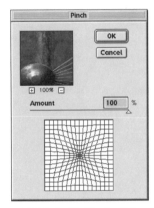

**FIGURE C–67** Pinch dialog box

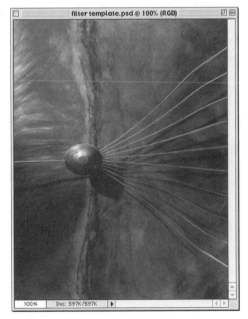

**FIGURE C–68** Pinch

## POLAR COORDINATES

This filter converts a selection from its rectangular coordinates to polar coordinates, and vice versa, according to the selected option. You can use it to create a cylinder anamorphosis—art popular in the 18th century—in which the distorted image appears normal when viewed in a mirrored cylinder (see Figures C–69 and C–70).

**FIGURE C–69** Polar Coordinates dialog box

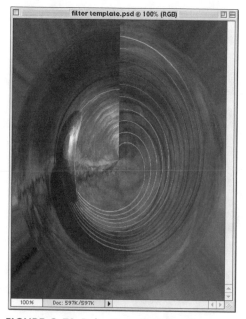

**FIGURE C–70** Polar Coordinates

## RIPPLE

The Ripple filter creates an undulating pattern on a selection, like ripples on the surface of a pond. For greater control, use the Wave filter. Options include the amount and size of ripples (see Figures C–71 and C–72).

**FIGURE C–71** Ripple dialog box

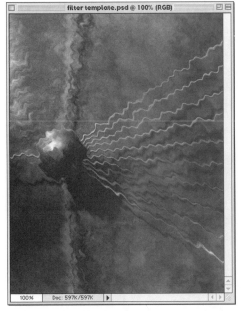

**FIGURE C–72** Ripple

## SHEAR

The Shear filter distorts an image along a curve. Specify the curve by dragging the line in the box to form a curve for the distortion. You can adjust any point along the curve. Click Defaults to return the curve to a straight line. In addition, you can choose how to treat undistorted areas (see Figures C–73 and C–74).

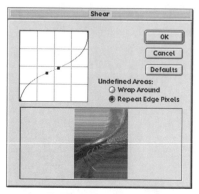

**FIGURE C–73** Shear dialog box

**FIGURE C–74** Shear

## SPHERIZE

The Spherize filter gives objects a 3-D effect by wrapping a selection around a spherical shape, distorting the image, and stretching it to fit the selected curve (see Figures C–75 and C–76).

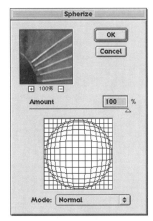

**FIGURE C–75** Spherize dialog box

**FIGURE C–76** Spherize

## TWIRL

The Twirl filter rotates a selection more sharply in the center than at the edges. Specifying an angle produces a twirl pattern (see Figures C–77 and C–78).

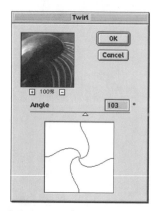

**FIGURE C–77** Twirl dialog box

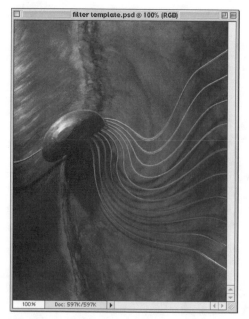

**FIGURE C–78** Twirl

## WAVE

The Wave filter works much like the Ripple filter, but with greater control. Adjustable options include the number of wave generators, the wavelength (distance from one wave crest to the next), the height of the wave, and the wave type: Sine (rolling), Triangle, or Square. The Randomize option applies random values. You can also define undistorted areas (see Figures C–79 and C–80).

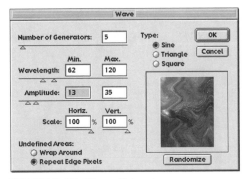

**FIGURE C–79** Wave dialog box

**FIGURE C–80** Wave

To replicate wave results on other selections, click Randomize, set the Number of Generators to 1, and set the minimum and maximum Wavelength and Amplitude parameters to the same value.

### ZIGZAG

The ZigZag filter distorts a selection radially, depending on the radius of the pixels in your selection. The Ridges option sets the number of direction reversals of the zigzag from the center of the selection to its edge. You also choose how to displace the pixels: The Pond Ripples option displaces pixels to the upper left or lower right; Out From Center displaces pixels toward or away from the center of the selection; and Around Center rotates pixels around the center (see Figures C–81 and C–82).

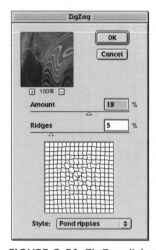

**FIGURE C–81** ZigZag dialog box

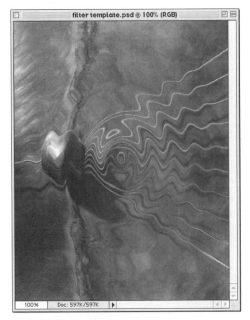

**FIGURE C–82** ZigZag

# ◆ Noise Filters

The Noise filters add or remove noise, or pixels with randomly distributed color levels. This helps to blend a selection into the surrounding pixels. Noise filters can create unusual textures or remove problem areas, such as dust and scratches, from an image.

### ADD NOISE

The Add Noise filter applies random pixels to an image, simulating the effect of shooting pictures on high-speed film. This filter can also be used to reduce banding in feathered selections or graduated fills, or to give a more realistic look to heavily retouched areas. Options include noise distribution: Uniform distributes color values of noise using random numbers between 0 and plus or minus the specified value, for a subtle effect; Gaussian distributes color values of noise along a bell-shaped curve for a speckled effect. The Monochromatic option applies the filter to only the tonal elements in the image without changing the colors (see Figures C–83 and C–84).

**FIGURE C–83** Add Noise dialog box

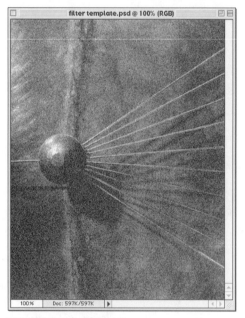

**FIGURE C–84** Add Noise

## DESPECKLE

The Despeckle filter detects the edges in an image (areas where significant color changes occur) and blurs all of the selection except those edges. This blurring removes noise while preserving detail (see Figure C–85).

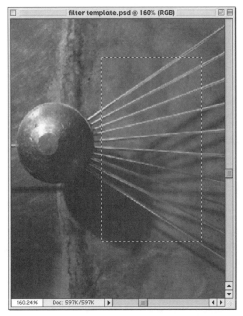

**FIGURE C–85** Despeckle

## DUST & SCRATCHES

This filter reduces noise by changing dissimilar pixels. To achieve a balance between sharpening the image and hiding defects, try various combinations of radius and threshold settings. Or apply the filter on selected areas in the image (see Figures C–86 and C–87).

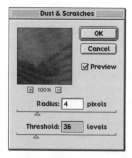

**FIGURE C–86** Dust & Scratches dialog box

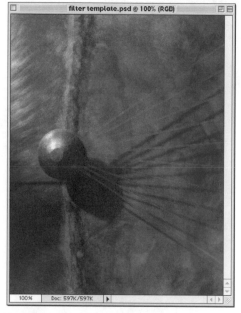

**FIGURE C–87** Dust & Scratches

To use the Dust & Scratches filter:

1. Choose Filter→Noise→Dust & Scratches.
2. If necessary, adjust the preview zoom ratio until the area containing noise is visible.
3. Drag the Threshold slider left to 0 to turn off the value, so that all pixels in the selection or image can be examined. The Threshold determines how different the pixels' values should be before they are eliminated. **Note:** The Threshold slider gives greater control for values between 0 and 128—the most common range for images—than for values between 128 and 255.
4. Drag the Radius slider left or right, or enter a value in the text box from 1 to 16 pixels. The Radius determines how far the filter searches for differences among pixels. Adjusting the radius makes the image blurry. Stop at the smallest value that eliminates the defects.
5. Increase the threshold gradually by entering a value or by dragging the slider to the highest value possible that eliminates defects.
6. Click OK.

## MEDIAN

The Median filter reduces noise in an image by blending the brightness of pixels within a selection. The filter searches the radius of a pixel selection for pixels of similar brightness, discarding pixels that differ too much from adjacent pixels, and replaces the center pixel with the median brightness value of the searched pixels. This filter is useful for eliminating or reducing the effect of motion on an image (see Figures C–88 and C–89).

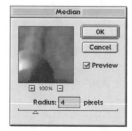

**FIGURE C–88** Median dialog box

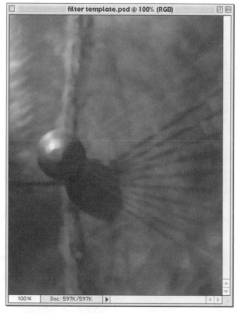

**FIGURE C–89** Median

# ◆ Pixelate Filters

The filters in the Pixelate submenu sharply define a selection by clumping pixels of similar color values in cells.

### COLOR HALFTONE

The Color Halftone filter simulates the effect of using an enlarged halftone screen on each channel of the image. For each channel, the filter divides the image into rectangles and replaces each rectangle with a circle. The circle size is proportional to the brightness of the rectangle (see Figures C–90 and C–91).

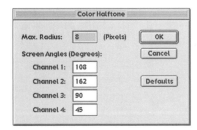

**FIGURE C–90** Color Halftone dialog box

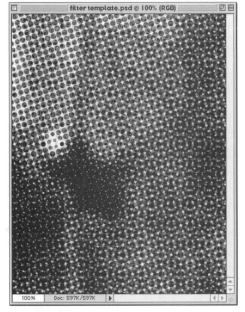

**FIGURE C–91** Color Halftone

To USE THE COLOR HALFTONE FILTER:

1.  Choose Filter→Pixelate→Color Halftone.
2.  Enter a value from 4 pixels to 127 pixels for the maximum radius of a halftone dot.
3.  Enter a screen-angle value (the angle of the dot from the true horizontal) for one or more channels:

    For Grayscale images, use only Channel 1.

    For RGB images, use Channels 1, 2, and 3, which correspond to the red, green, and blue channels, respectively.

    For CMYK images, use all four channels, which correspond to the cyan, magenta, yellow, and black channels.

    Click Defaults to return all the screen angles to their default values.
4.  Click OK.

## CRYSTALLIZE

The Crystallize filter clumps pixels into a solid color in a polygonal shape (see Figures C–92 and C–93).

**FIGURE C–92** Crystallize dialog box

**FIGURE C–93** Crystallize

## FACET

The Facet filter clumps pixels of solid or similar colors into blocks of like-colored pixels. You can use this filter to make a scanned image look hand-painted, or to make a realistic image resemble an abstract painting (see Figure C–94).

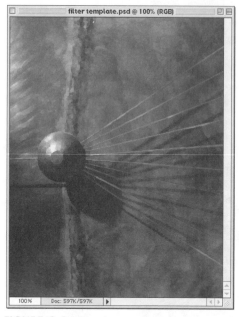

**FIGURE C–94** Facet

## FRAGMENT

The Fragment filter creates four copies of the pixels in the selection, averages them, and offsets them from each other (see Figure C–95).

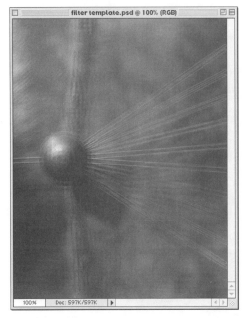

**FIGURE C–95** Fragment

## MEZZOTINT

This filter converts an image to a random pattern of black-and-white areas or of fully saturated colors in a color image. To use the filter, choose a dot pattern from the Type pop-up menu in the Mezzotint dialog box (see Figures C–96 and C–97).

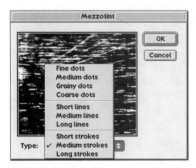

**FIGURE C–96** Mezzotint dialog box

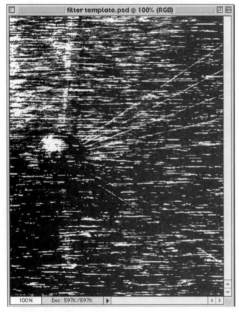

**FIGURE C–97** Mezzotint

## MOSAIC

The Mosaic filter clumps pixels into square blocks. The pixels in a given block are the same color, and the colors of the blocks represent the colors in the selection (see Figures C–98 and C–99).

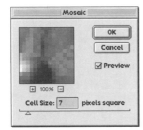

**FIGURE C–98** Mosaic dialog box

**FIGURE C–99** Mosaic

## POINTILLIZE

The Pointillize filter breaks up the color in an image into randomly placed dots, as in a pointillist painting, and uses the background color as a canvas area between the dots (see Figures C–100 and C–101).

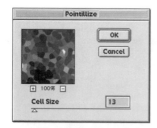

**FIGURE C–100** Pointillize dialog box

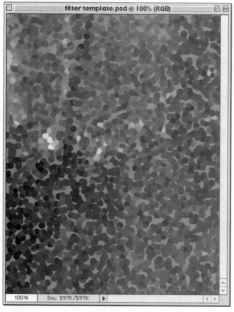

**FIGURE C–101** Pointillize

# ◆ Render Filters

The Render filters create 3-D shapes, cloud patterns, refraction patterns, and simulated light reflections in an image. You can also manipulate objects in 3-D space, create 3-D objects (cubes, spheres, and cylinders), and create texture fills from grayscale files to produce 3D-like effects for lighting.

### 3D TRANSFORM

This filter maps images to cubes, spheres, and cylinders, which you can then rotate in three dimensions (see Figures C–102 through C–104).

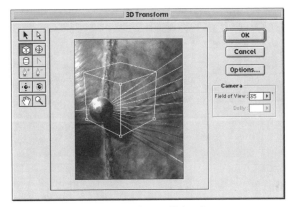

**FIGURE C–102** 3D Transform dialog box

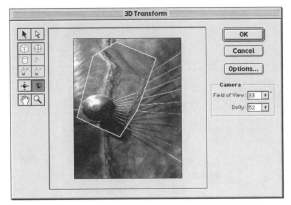

**FIGURE C–103** 3D Transform dialog box number 2

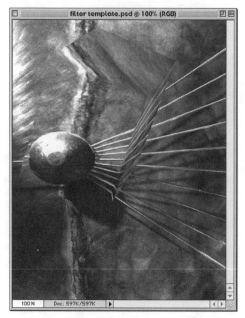

**FIGURE C–104** 3D Transform

## CLOUDS

This filter generates a soft cloud pattern using random values that vary between the foreground and the background colors. To generate a more stark cloud pattern, hold down the Alt key (on a PC) or the Option key (on a Mac) as you choose Filter→Render→Clouds (see Figure C–105).

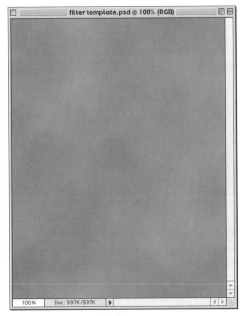

**FIGURE C–105** Clouds

## DIFFERENCE CLOUDS

This filter uses randomly generated values that vary between the foreground and background color to produce a cloud pattern. The filter blends the cloud data with the existing pixels in the same way that the Difference mode blends colors. The first time you choose this filter, portions of the image are inverted in a cloud pattern. Applying the filter several times creates rib and vein patterns that resemble a marble texture (see Figure C–106).

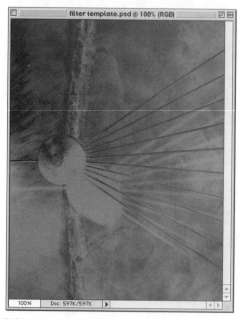

**FIGURE C–106** Difference Clouds

### LENS FLARE

The Lens Flare filter simulates the refraction caused by shining a bright light into the camera lens. Specify a location for the center of the flare by clicking anywhere inside the image thumbnail or by dragging its crosshair (see Figures C–107 and C–108).

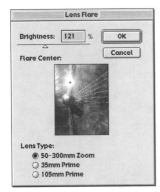

**FIGURE C–107** Lens Flare dialog box

**FIGURE C–108** Lens Flare

## LIGHTING EFFECTS

This filter lets you produce myriad lighting effects on RGB images by varying 17 light styles, 3 light types, and 4 sets of light properties. You can also use textures from grayscale files (called *bump maps*) to produce 3D-like effects and save your own styles for use in other images (see Figures C–109 and C–110).

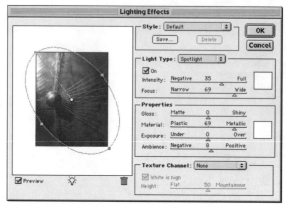

**FIGURE C–109** Lighting Effects dialog box

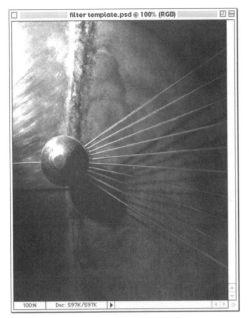

**FIGURE C–110** Lighting Effects

## TEXTURE FILL

This filter fills a selection with a grayscale file or part of a file. To add texture to the document or selection, open the grayscale document you want to use as the texture fill (see Figures C–111 and C–112).

**FIGURE C–111** Texture Fill—Texture to be used

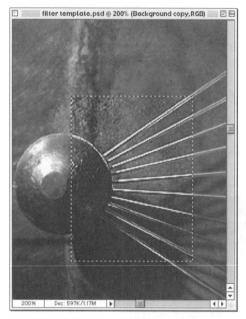

**FIGURE C–114** Sharpen More

## SHARPEN EDGES

This filter finds the areas in the image where significant color changes occur and sharpens them. The Sharpen Edges filter sharpens only edges while preserving the overall smoothness of the image. Use this filter to sharpen edges without specifying an amount (see Figure 115).

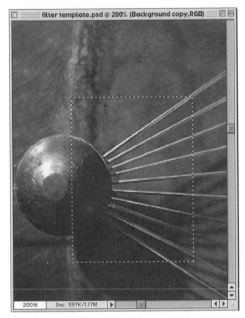

**FIGURE C–115** Sharpen Edges

## UNSHARP MASK

The Unsharp Mask filter locates pixels that differ from surrounding pixels by the threshold you specify and increases the pixels' contrast by the amount you specify. In addition, you can specify the radius of the region to which each pixel is compared (see Figures C–116 and C–117).

**FIGURE C–116** Unsharp Mask dialog box

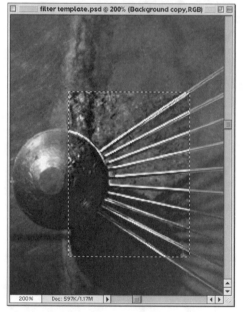

**FIGURE C–117** Unsharp Mask

The effects of the Unsharp Mask filter are far more pronounced onscreen than in high-resolution output. If your final destination is print, experiment to determine what dialog box settings work best for your image.

To sharpen an image using the Unsharp Mask filter:

1. Choose Filter→Sharpen→Unsharp Mask.
2. Sharpen the image:
   - For Amount, drag the slider or enter a value to determine how much to increase the contrast of pixels. For high-resolution printed images, an amount between 150% and 200% is recommended.
   - For Radius, drag the slider or enter a value to determine the number of pixels surrounding the edge pixels that affects the sharpening. For high-resolution images, a Radius between 1 and 2 is recommended.
     - A lower value sharpens only the edge pixels, whereas a higher value sharpens a wider band of pixels. This effect is much less noticeable in print than onscreen, because a 2-pixel radius represents a smaller area in a high-resolution printed image.
   - For Threshold, drag the slider or enter a value to determine how different the sharpened pixels must be from the surrounding area before they are considered edge pixels and sharpened by the filter. To avoid introducing noise (in images with fleshtones, for example), experiment with Threshold values between 2 and 20. The default Threshold value (0) sharpens all pixels in the image.

# ◆ Sketch Filters

Filters in the Sketch submenu add texture to images, often for a 3-D effect. The filters are also useful for creating a fine-arts or hand-drawn look. Many of the Sketch filters use the foreground and background colors as they redraw the image.

## BAS RELIEF

The Bas Relief filter transforms an image to appear carved in low relief and lit to accent the surface variations. Dark areas of the image take on the foreground color; light colors use the background color (see Figures C–118 and C–119).

**FIGURE C–118** Bas Relief dialog box

**FIGURE C–119** Bas Relief

## CHALK & CHARCOAL

This filter redraws an image's highlights and midtones with a solid, midtone gray background drawn in coarse chalk. Shadow areas are replaced with black, diagonal charcoal lines. The charcoal is drawn in the foreground color, the chalk is drawn in the background color (see Figures C–120 and C–121).

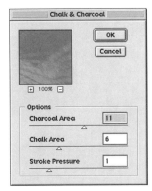

**FIGURE C–120** Chalk & Charcoal dialog box

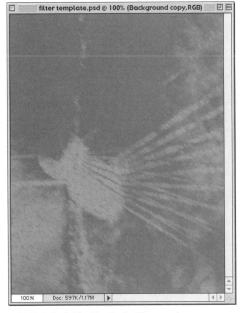

**FIGURE C–121** Chalk & Charcoal

## CHARCOAL

This filter redraws an image to create a posterized, smudged effect. Major edges are boldly drawn, while midtones are sketched using a diagonal stroke. Charcoal is the foreground color, and the paper is the background color (see Figures C–122 and C–123).

**FIGURE C–122** Charcoal dialog box

**FIGURE C–123** Charcoal

## CHROME

The Chrome filter treats the image as if it were a polished chrome surface. Highlights are high points and shadows are low points in the reflecting surface. After applying the filter, use the Levels dialog box to add more contrast to the image (see Figures C–124 and C–125).

**FIGURE C–124** Chrome dialog box

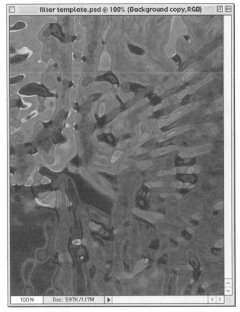

**FIGURE C–125** Chrome

## CONTÉ CRAYON

This filter replicates the texture of dense dark and pure white Conté crayons on an image. It uses the foreground color for dark areas and the background color for light areas. For a truer effect, change the foreground color to one of the common Conté Crayon colors (black, sepia, sanguine) before applying the filter. For a muted effect, change the background color to white with some foreground color added to it before applying the filter (see Figures C–126 and C–127).

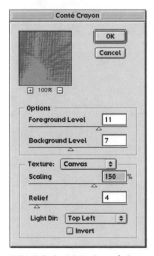

**FIGURE C–126** Conté Crayon dialog box

**FIGURE C–127** Conté Crayon

## GRAPHIC PEN

The Graphic Pen filter uses fine, linear ink strokes to capture the details in the original image, and is especially striking with scanned images. The filter replaces color in the original image using the foreground color for ink and background color for paper (see Figures C–128 and C–129).

**FIGURE C–128** Graphic Pen dialog box

**FIGURE C–129** Graphic Pen

## HALFTONE SCREEN

This filter simulates the effect of a halftone screen while maintaining the continuous range of tones (see Figures C–130 and C–131).

**FIGURE C–130** Halftone Screen dialog box

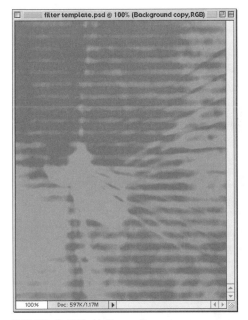

**FIGURE C–131** Halftone Screen

## NOTE PAPER

Note Paper creates an image that appears to be constructed of handmade paper. The filter simplifies an image, and combines the effects of the Texture, Emboss, and Grain filters. Dark areas of the image appear as holes in the top layer of paper, revealing the background color (see Figures C–132 and C–133).

**FIGURE C–132** Note Paper dialog box

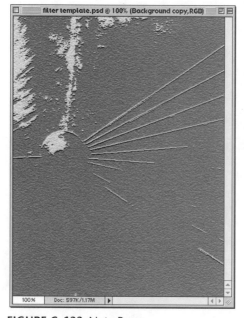

**FIGURE C–133** Note Paper

## PHOTOCOPY

This filter simulates the effect of photocopying an image. Large areas of darkness tend to copy only around their edges, and midtones fall away to either solid black or white (see Figures C–134 and C–135).

**FIGURE C–134** Photocopy dialog box

**FIGURE C–135** Photocopy

## PLASTER

This filter molds an image from 3-D plaster, and then colorizes the result using the foreground and background colors. Dark areas are raised, light areas are sunken (or reverse the effect by choosing the Invert option) (see Figures C–136 and C–137).

**FIGURE C–136** Plaster dialog box

**FIGURE C–137** Plaster

## RETICULATION

This filter simulates the controlled shrinking and distorting of film emulsion to create an image that appears clumped in the shadows and lightly grained in the highlights (see Figures C–138 and C–139).

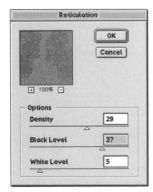

**FIGURE C–138** Reticulation dialog box

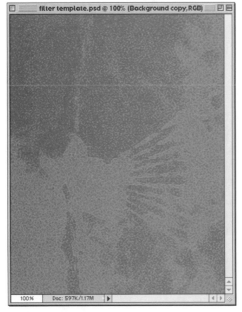

**FIGURE C–139** Reticulation

## STAMP

The Stamp filter is best used with black-and-white images. The filter simplifies the image to appear stamped with a rubber or wood stamp (see Figures C–140 and C–141).

**FIGURE C–140** Stamp dialog box

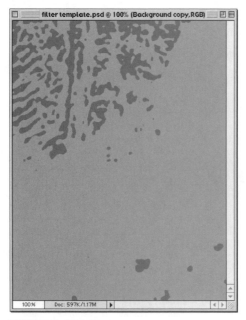

**FIGURE C–141** Stamp

## TORN EDGES

The Torn Edges filter is particularly useful for images consisting of text or high-contrast objects. It reconstructs the image as ragged, torn pieces of paper, and then colorizes the image using the foreground and background colors (see Figures C–142 and C–143).

**FIGURE C–142** Torn Edges dialog box

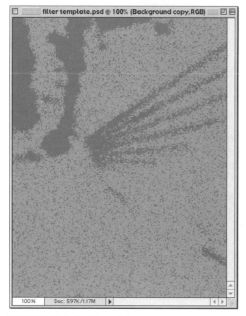

**FIGURE C–143** Torn Edges

## WATER PAPER

The Water Paper filter uses blotchy daubs that appear painted onto fibrous, damp paper, causing the colors to flow and blend (see Figures C–144 and C–145).

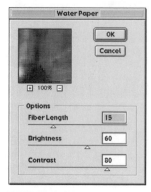

**FIGURE C–144** Water Paper dialog box

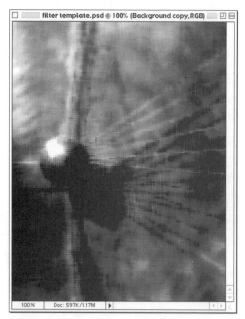

**FIGURE C–145** Water Paper

# ◆ Stylize Filters

The Stylize filters produce a painted or impressionistic effect on a selection by displacing pixels and by finding and heightening contrast in an image. After using filters like Find Edges and Trace Contour, which highlight edges, you can apply the Invert command to outline the edges of a color image with colored lines or to outline the edges of a grayscale image with white lines.

### DIFFUSE

The Diffuse filter shuffles pixels in a selection to make the selection look less focused according to the selected option: Normal moves pixels randomly, ignoring color values; Darken Only replaces light pixels with darker pixels; and Lighten Only replaces dark pixels with lighter pixels (see Figures C–146 and C–147).

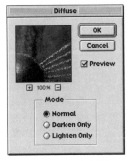

**FIGURE C–146** Diffuse dialog box

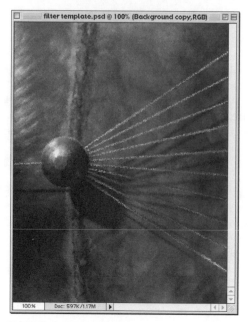

**FIGURE C–147** Diffuse

## EMBOSS

This filter makes a selection appear raised or stamped by converting its fill color to gray and tracing the edges with the original fill color. Options include an embossing angle (from –360° to lower (stamp) the surface, to +360° to raise the surface); height; and a percentage (1% to 500%) for the amount of color within the selection. To retain color and detail when embossing, use the Fade command after applying the Emboss filter (see Figures C–148 and C–149).

**FIGURE C–148** Emboss dialog box

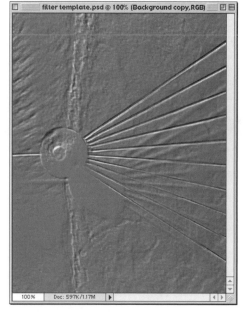

**FIGURE C–149** Emboss

## EXTRUDE

The Extrude filter gives a 3-D texture to a selection or layer (see Figures C–150 and C–151).

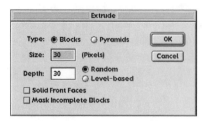

**FIGURE C–150** Extrude dialog box

**FIGURE C–151** Extrude

To use the Extrude filter:

1. Choose Filter→Stylize→Extrude.
2. Choose a 3-D object:
   - The Blocks option lets you create objects with a square front face and four side faces. To fill the front face of each block with the average color of the block, select the Solid Front Faces option. To fill the front face with the image, keep the Solid Front Faces option deselected.
   - The Pyramids option lets you create objects with four triangular sides that meet at a point.
3. Enter a value from 2 to 255 in the Size text box to determine the length of any side of the object's base.
4. Enter a value from 0 to 255 in the Depth text box to indicate how far the tallest object appears to protrude from the screen.
5. Choose a Depth option:
   - Random gives each block or pyramid an arbitrary depth.
   - Level-based makes each object's depth correspond to its brightness—bright protrudes more than dark.
6. Select Mask Incomplete Blocks to hide any object extending beyond the selection.
7. Click OK.

## FIND EDGES

This filter identifies the areas of the image with significant transitions and emphasizes the edges. Like the Trace Counter filter, Find Edges outlines the edges of an image with dark lines against a white background and is useful for creating a border around an image (see Figure C–152).

**FIGURE C–152** Find Edges

## GLOWING EDGES

The Glowing Edges filter identifies the edges of color and adds a neon-like glow to them (see Figures C–153 and C–154).

**FIGURE C–153** Glowing Edges dialog box

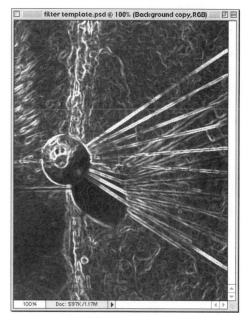

**FIGURE C–154** Glowing Edges

## SOLARIZE

The Solarize filter blends a negative and a positive image—similar to exposing a photographic print briefly to light during development (see Figure C–155).

**FIGURE C–155** Solarize

## TILES

This filter breaks up an image into a series of tiles, offsetting the selection from its original position. You can choose to fill the area between the tiles with the background color; the foreground color; an inverse version of the image; or an unaltered version of the image, which puts the tiled version of the image on top of the original and reveals part of the original image underneath the tiled edges (see Figures C–156 and C–157).

**FIGURE C–156** Tiles dialog box

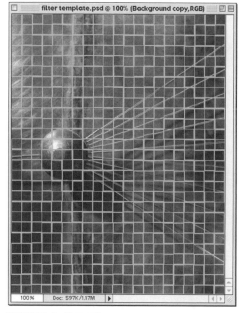

**FIGURE C–157** Tiles

## TRACE CONTOUR

This filter finds the transitions of major brightness areas and thinly outlines them for each color channel for an effect similar to the lines in a contour map (see Figures C–158 and C–159).

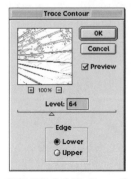

**FIGURE C–158** Trace Contour dialog box

**FIGURE C–159** Trace Contour

To use the Trace Contour filter:

1. Choose Filter→Stylize→Trace Contour.
2. Choose an Edge option to outline areas in the selection: Lower outlines where the color values of pixels fall below the specified level; Upper outlines where the color values are above the specified level.
3. Enter a threshold (Level) from 0 to 255 for evaluating color values (tonal level). Experiment to see what values bring out the best detail in the image. Use the Info palette in Grayscale mode to identify a color value that you want traced. Then, enter the value in the Level text box.
4. Click OK.

## WIND

The Wind filter creates tiny, horizontal lines in the image to simulate a wind effect. Methods include Wind; Blast, for a more dramatic wind effect; and Stagger, which offsets the wind lines in the image (see Figures C–160 and C–161).

**FIGURE C–160** Wind dialog box

**FIGURE C–161** Wind

# ◆ Texture Filters

Use the Texture filters to give an image the appearance of depth or substance, or to add an organic look.

### CRAQUELURE

The Craquelure filter paints an image onto a high-relief plaster surface, producing a fine network of cracks that follow the contours of the image. Use this filter to create an embossing effect with images that contain a broad range of color or grayscale values (see Figures C–162 and C–163).

**FIGURE C–162** Craquelure dialog box

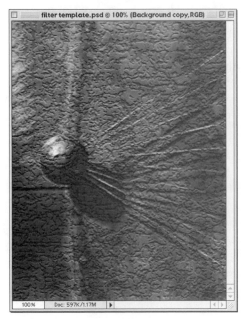

**FIGURE C–163** Craquelure

## GRAIN

Grain adds texture to an image by simulating different kinds of grain—regular, soft, sprinkles, clumped, contrasty, enlarged, stippled, horizontal, vertical, and speckle (see Figures C–164 and C–165).

**FIGURE C–164**  Grain dialog box

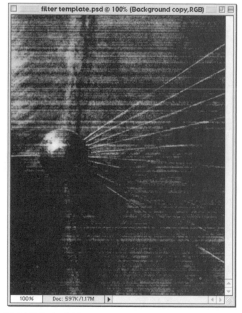

**FIGURE C–165**  Grain

## MOSAIC TILES

This filter draws the image as if it had been made up of small chips or tiles and adds grout between the tiles. (In contrast, the Pixelate→Mosaic filter breaks up an image into blocks of different colored pixels.) (see Figures C–166 and C–167.)

**FIGURE C–166** Mosaic Tiles dialog box

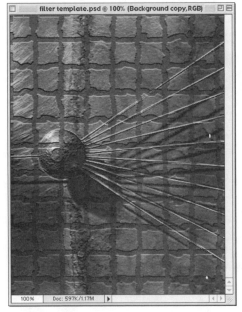

**FIGURE C–167** Mosaic Tiles

## PATCHWORK

The Patchwork filter breaks up an image into squares filled with the predominant color in that area of the image. The filter randomly reduces or increases the tile depth to replicate the highlights and shadows (see Figures C–168 and C–169).

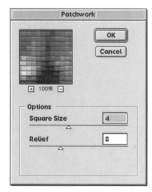

**FIGURE C–168** Patchwork dialog box

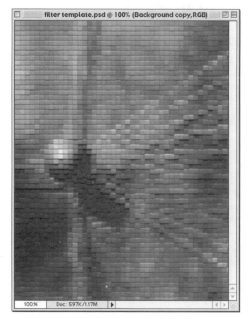

**FIGURE C–169** Patchwork

## STAINED GLASS

This filter repaints an image as single-colored adjacent cells outlined in the foreground color (see Figures C–170 and C–171).

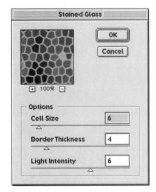

**FIGURE C–170** Stained Glass dialog box

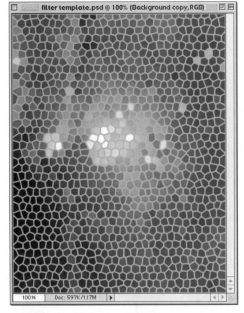

**FIGURE C–171** Stained Glass

## TEXTURIZER

The Texturizer filter applies a texture you select or create to an image (see Figures C–172 and C–173).

**FIGURE C–172** Texturizer dialog box

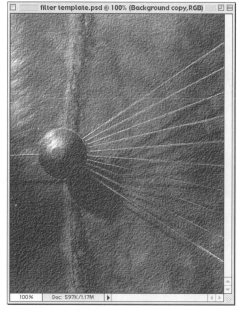

**FIGURE C–173** Texturizer

# ◆ Video Filters

This is a Web book, not a video book. You don't need these filters, but here are some pictures anyway.

### DE-INTERLACE

De-Interlace smoothes moving images captured on video by removing either the odd or even interlaced lines in a video image. You can choose to replace the discarded lines by duplication or interpolation (see Figures C–174 and C–175).

**FIGURE C–174** De-Interlace dialog box

**FIGURE C–175** De-Interlace

### NTSC COLORS

This filter restricts the gamut of colors to those acceptable for television reproduction to prevent oversaturated colors from bleeding across television scan lines.

# ◆ Other Filters

Filters in the Other submenu let you create your own filters, use filters to modify masks, offset a selection within an image, and make quick color adjustments.

### CUSTOM

The Custom filter lets you design your own filter effect. With the Custom filter, you can change the brightness values of each pixel in the image according to a predefined mathematical operation known as *convolution*. Each pixel is reassigned a value based on the values of surrounding pixels. This operation is similar to the Add and Subtract calculations for channels.

You can save the custom filters you create and use them with other Adobe Photoshop images.

#### TO CREATE A CUSTOM FILTER:

1. Choose Filter→Other→Custom.
2. Select the center text box, which represents the pixel being evaluated. Enter a value from –999 to +999 by which you want to multiply that pixel's brightness value.
3. Select a text box representing an adjacent pixel. Enter the value by which you want the pixel in this position multiplied. For example, to multiply the brightness value of the pixel to the immediate right of the current pixel by 2, enter 2 in the text box to the immediate right of the center text box.
4. Repeat steps 2 and 3 for all pixels to include in the operation. You don't have to enter values in all the text boxes.
5. For Scale, enter the value by which you want to divide the sum of the brightness values of the pixels included in the calculation.
6. For Offset, enter the value to be added to the result of the scale calculation.

Click OK. The custom filter is applied to each pixel in the image, one at a time. Use the Save and Load buttons to save and reuse custom filters (see Figures C–176 and C–177).

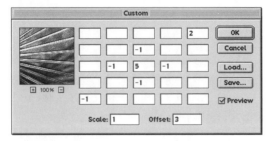

FIGURE C–176  Custom dialog box

FIGURE C–177  Custom

## HIGH PASS

The High Pass filter retains edge details in the specified radius where sharp color transitions occur and suppresses the rest of the image (A radius of 0.1 pixel keeps only edge pixels.) The filter removes low-frequency detail in an image, and has the opposite effect of the Gaussian Blur filter.

It is helpful to apply the High Pass filter to a continuous-tone image before using the Threshold command or converting the image to Bitmap mode. The filter is useful for extracting line art and large black-and-white areas from scanned images (see Figures C–178 and C–179).

**FIGURE C–178** High Pass dialog box

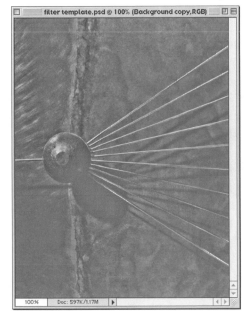

**FIGURE C–179** High Pass

## MINIMUM AND MAXIMUM

These filters are useful for modifying masks. The Minimum filter has the effect of applying a spread—spreading out black areas and shrinking white areas. The Maximum filter has the effect of applying a choke—spreading out white areas and choking in black areas. Like the Median filter, the Minimum and Maximum filters look at individual pixels in a selection. Within a specified radius, the Minimum and Maximum filters replace the current pixel's brightness value with the greatest or least brightness value of the surrounding pixels (see Figures C–180 through C–183).

**FIGURE C–180** Minimum dialog box

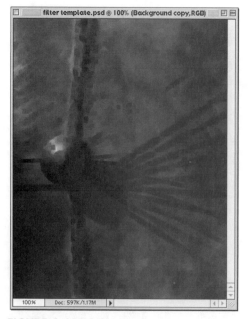

**FIGURE C–181** Minimum

**FIGURE C–182** Maximum dialog box

**FIGURE C–183** Maximum

## OFFSET

The Offset filter moves a selection a specified horizontal or vertical amount, leaving an empty space at the selection's original location. You can fill the empty area with the current background color, with another part of the image, or with your choice of fill if the selection is near the edge of an image (see Figures C–184 and C–185).

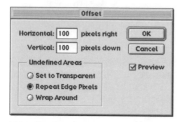

**FIGURE C–184** Offset dialog box

**FIGURE C–185** Offset

# Index

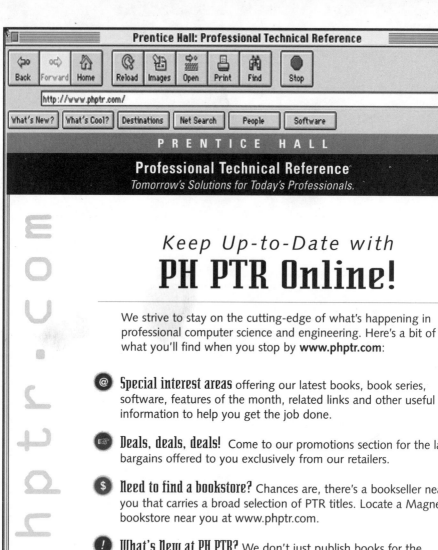